本成果受到中国人民大学2018年度
“中央高校建设世界一流大学（学科）和特色发展引导专项资金”支持

光伏补贴政策设计与评估

以美国加州为例

PV Subsidy Policy Design and Evaluation
A Case Study of California

董长贵◎著

知识产权出版社
全国百佳图书出版单位

图书在版编目（CIP）数据

光伏补贴政策设计与评估——以美国加州为例 = PV Subsidy Policy Design and Evaluation: A Case Study of California : 英文 / 董长贵著 . —北京 : 知识产权出版社，2019.4

ISBN 978-7-5130-6221-3

Ⅰ.①光… Ⅱ.①董… Ⅲ.①太阳能发电—技术推广—研究—美国—英文 ②太阳能发电—电力工业—政府补贴—财政政策—研究—美国—英文 Ⅳ.① F471.266 ② F817.120

中国版本图书馆 CIP 数据核字（2019）第 075179 号

内容提要

本书以作者的博士论文为基础，聚焦于技术扩散基本理论和新型技术政府补贴政策的设计和评估，以美国光伏太阳能行业发展最好的加州为例，介绍了加州政府的光伏补贴政策、设计基本原则和过程以及政策的最终实施效果，并从补贴政策优化设计和补贴转嫁效应两个视角透视加州的光伏补贴政策。本研究发现美国加州的光伏补贴政策通过引入灵活性机制设计，很好地处理了光伏技术快速进步所带来的成本和价格不确定性；另外，在补贴转嫁效应方面，研究发现政府的补贴几乎全额被消费者获得，因此政策取得了良好的效果。本研究对于优化我国的光伏补贴政策、补贴类似新型技术（如风能、电动车、电池技术）等相关问题有重要的启示和借鉴意义。

责任编辑：荆成恭　陈晶晶　　**责任校对：**谷　洋
装帧设计：李志伟　　**责任印制：**孙婷婷

光伏补贴政策设计与评估
——以美国加州为例
PV Subsidy Policy Design and Evaluation: A Case Study of California
董长贵　著

出版发行：知识产权出版社有限责任公司	**网　　址：**http://www.ipph.cn
社　　址：北京市海淀区气象路 50 号院	**邮　　编：**100081
责编电话：010-82000860 转 8391	**责编邮箱：**shiny-chjj@163.com
发行电话：010-82000860 转 8101/8102	**发行传真：**010-82000893/82005070/82000270
印　　刷：北京虎彩文化传播有限公司	**经　　销：**各大网上书店、新华书店及相关专业书店
开　　本：720mm × 1000mm　1/16	**印　　张：**10.5
版　　次：2019 年 4 月第 1 版	**印　　次：**2019 年 4 月第 1 次印刷
字　　数：208 千字	**定　　价：**59.00 元

ISBN 978-7-5130-6221-3

Preface

Human-induced climate change, with its potentially catastrophic impacts on weather patterns, water resources, ecosystems, and agricultural production, is the toughest global problem of modern times. One of the 2018 Nobel Prize winner in economic science—William Nordhaus is awarded for his economic analysis of climate change. Impeding catastrophic climate change necessitates the widespread deployment of renewable energy technologies for reducing the emissions of heat-trapping gases, especially carbon dioxide(CO_2). However, the deployment of renewable energy technologies is plagued by various market failures, such as environmental externalities from fossil fuels, technology learning-by-doing, innovation spillover effects, and peer effects. In efforts to address these market failures, governments at all levels—city, state, regional, and national—have instituted various subsidies for promoting the adoption of renewable energy technologies. Since public resources are limited and have competing uses, it is important to ask: how cost-effective are renewable energy subsidies? And are the subsidies even reaching the intended recipients—the adopters of renewable energy technologies? In this book, I choose to answer these two research questions with a focus on the biggest solar subsidy programs in California.

On cost-effectiveness, all programs to incentivize the adoption of renewable energy technologies run into the same key question: what is the optimal rebate schedule in the face of volatile product prices and the need for policy certainty?

Answering this question requires careful attentions to both supply-side(learning-by-doing) and demand-side(peer effects) market dynamics. Then I use dynamic programming to analyze the effectiveness of the largest state-level solar PV subsidy program in the U.S.—the California Solar Initiative(CSI)—in maximizing the cumulative PV installation in California under a budget constraint. I find that previous studies overestimated learning-by-doing in the solar industry. Consistent with other studies, I also find that peer effects are a significant demand driver in the California solar market. The main implication of this empirical finding in the dynamic optimization context is that it forces the optimal solution towards higher subsidies in earlier years of the program, and, hence, leads to a lower program duration(for the same budget). In particular, I find that the optimal rebate schedule would start not at \$2.5/W as it actually did in CSI, but instead at \$4.2/W; the effective policy period would be only three years instead of the realized period of six years. This optimal(i.e., most cost effective) solution results in total PV adoption of 32.2MW(8.1%) higher than that installed under CSI, while using the same budget. Furthermore, I find that the optimal rebate schedule starts to look like the implemented CSI in a "policy certainty" scenario where the variation of periodic subsidy-level changes is constrained, and thus creating policy certainty. Finally, introduction of stochastic learning-by-doing as a way to better capture the dynamic nature of learning in markets for new products does not yield significantly different results compared to the deterministic case.

Another key question related to the redistribution effect of the CSI program is: to what degree have the direct PV incentives in California been passed through from installers to PV customers? I address this question by carefully examining the residential PV market in California with multiple quantitative methods. Specifically, I apply a structural-modeling approach, a reduced-form regression analysis, and regression discontinuity designs to estimate the incentive pass-through rate for the CSI. The results consistently show a high average pass-through rate of direct incentives of nearly 100%, though with regional differences among California counties and utilities. While these results could have multiple explanations, they suggest a relatively competitive market and a smoothly operating subsidy program.

Combining evidence from the optimal subsidy policy design and the incentive pass-through analysis, this research lends credibility to the cost-effectiveness of CSI given CSI's design goal of providing policy certainty and also finds a near-perfect incidence in CSI. Long-term credible commitment as reflected through CSI's capacity-triggered step changes in rebates along with policy and data transparency are important factors for CSI's smooth and cost-effective functioning. Though CSI has now wound down because final solar capacity targets have been reached, the performance of CSI is relevant not only as an ex-post analysis in California, but potentially has broader policy implications for other solar incentive programs in other states and countries such as China.

This book is a reprint of my Ph.D dissertation at the University of Texas at Austin back in 2014. Although four years have passed since then, much of its content is still relevant for readers in China. Firstly, it shows how a serious Ph.D dissertation in the United States looks like, from which one might guess how many efforts are involved behind. Secondly, by comparing it to more recent literature(mostly working papers), the observations and conclusions made in my dissertation still stand correct. For example, more and more papers start to show that the incentive pass-through rate for solar photovoltaic(PV) subsidy programs is high or complete, though at first sight this conclusion may seem odd to some people. Thirdly, since PV subsidies have played a key role in promoting China to be the world-largest PV market, more research should be conducted on China's PV subsidies in the terms of policy evaluation and potential adjustment. For instance, how to avoid the sudden change of "530-policy" in China? In all three aspects, this book can be taken as a good starting point.

While preparing this manuscript, I would like to acknowledge those who have helped me along the way. Firstly, I am grateful to have Dr. Varun Rai join in the LBJ School at the University of Texas at Austin, then become my advisor and inspire many of my ideas. His generous help and unlimited support have encouraged me to try different approaches to answering important questions. We have shared very long working hours on meeting deadlines together, and discussed research and teaching philosophy, among other things, during our shared road trips to Houston, Texas. I also want to thank Dr. Kenneth Flamm to enroll me and be my academic advisor at the beginning. I am awe-inspired by his extraordinary knowledge of the semiconductor industry, and I in particular acknowledge his financial support for my research during the first few years after I came to the U.S. My sincere thanks go to Dean Chandler Stolp, a great mentor and teacher, who helped me tremendously during my transition to doctoral candidacy. I would also love to thank Dr. Jay Zarnikau for his valuable and timely feedback on several of my papers, Dr. Ross Baldick for his passion about everything and generosity with his time to discuss things with me, and Dr. Eric Bickel for pushing me to make my dissertation more and more rigorous.

I have bothered many people for help with editing, and I would like to thank all of them here, including Carlos Olmedo, Jarett Zuboy, Vivek Nath, Ariane Beck, Trevor Udwin, Erik Funkhouser, Matthew Stringer, Cale Reeves, and Tobin McKearin. I also want to thank Scott Robinson for his GIS help along the way.

Dr. Ryan Wiser from the Lawrence Berkeley National Laboratory(LBNL) has helped me a lot for not only funding me to conduct part of my dissertation research, but also providing me his many insights on the solar PV industry. Naim Darghouth and Galen Barbose, both from LBNL, have helped me a lot to get to know their data.

I thank China Scholarship Council for their financial support during my Ph.D life, and thank my Chinese colleges here at UT Austin, Liangfei Qiu, Hao Hang, Fang Tang, Zhu Chen, Yumin Li, and Zhufeng Gao for making my Ph.D life more colorful.

Lastly, I would like to thank my then-girlfriend and now wife, Fang Cong, for her love and support through my Ph.D life; without her, I probably will finish my dissertation a couple of months earlier. Also, I want to thank my family for fully supporting me going abroad and forgiving me for not being around.

The publication of this work has been supported by the MOF and MOE specific fund of "Building World-Class Universities(Disciplines) and Fostering characteristic Development" received by Renmin University of China in 2018. The author would also like to acknowledge the help from editor Jingjing Chen and editor Chenggong Jing at the Intellectual Property Publishing House Co., Ltd. Their editing has made this book more readable.

Contents

List of Tables

List of Figures

Chapter 1 Introduction

Human-induced climate change, with its potentially catastrophic impacts on weather patterns, water resources, ecosystems, and agricultural production(IPCC WG2, 2014), is the toughest global problem of modern times(Dow and Downing, 2011). Based on the latest projection by the Intergovernmental Panel on Climate Change(IPCC), global surface temperature has been increasing almost linearly in the past four decades or so, and the temperature change is highly likely to exceed 2℃ by the end of the 21st century(IPCC WG1, 2014). Such change is likely to cause significant global GDP losses; the well-known Stern Report(Stern, 2007) estimated that for a global mean temperature change of 2℃~3℃, the potential global GDP loss would be around 1%~2%. This number may look small, however, no single country wishes to bear the burden alone.

While the concentration of greenhouse gases(GHGs) from the human activities is the largest driver of the observed climate change(EPA, 2014a), tracing the sources of GHGs reveals that in the United States, electricity generation produces the largest share of GHGs. In 2012, this sector emits 32% of GHGs in the United States, followed by the transportation sector at 28%(EPA, 2014b). Obviously, different electricity generation technologies tend to have very different emission rates. Based on a recent review report(WNA, 2011) that summarizes life-cycle assessments of the GHG emission intensity for different generation technologies, solar photovoltaic(PV)① only emits 85 tons of CO_2e per GWh, while the numbers

---

① Solar PV—belonging to a broader set of solar energy technologies that also includes solar heating and cooling and concentrating solar power—converts sunlight to electricity using photovoltaic cells that are made of silicon or other crystalline compounds.

for natural gas and coal are 500 and 888 respectively.①

Unfortunately, electricity generation costs do not necessarily reflect the differences among technologies in terms of GHG emission intensity, within a market where there is no price for carbon or GHGs. This is the so-called environmental externality problem, i.e. the GHG emitters do not need to pay for the environmental damages that they cause. A natural cure for this externality problem is to put a price on carbon or all GHGs, i.e. a Pigovian tax(Pigou, 1920). Nevertheless, few countries have chosen this path; instead, most of them have come to support renewable energy technologies directly. As pointed out in the IPCC mitigation report, impeding catastrophic climate change necessitates the widespread deployment of renewable energy technologies for reducing the emissions of heat-trapping gases, especially carbon di-oxide(CO_2)(IPCC WG3, 2014).

The solar PV industry has been growing very rapidly in the last decade. According to the International Energy Agency(IEA), since 2000 solar PV has had the fastest growth rate among renewable energy technologies worldwide(IEA, 2010). While the global annual installed PV capacity was less than 0.3 gigawatts(GW) in 2000, this number surpassed 38GW in 2013(EPIA, 2014). Reflecting the rapid growth in deployment, global investment in solar energy technologies has been over $100 billion since 2000(Statista, 2014). Deployment in the United States has also grown rapidly from around 0.004GW of newly installed capacity in 2000 to more than 4GW installed in 2013 alone(Sherwood, 2013; SEIA/GTM, 2014).

A key driving force behind the growth of solar PV has been the myriad of government incentive programs promoting solar deployment(Arvizu et al., 2011; Kirkegaard et al., 2010; REN21, 2014; Timilsina et al., 2011), often motivated by a desire to address various market failures such as: environmental externalities as mentioned above(Baumol and Oates, 1988; Bezdek, 1993; Painuly, 2002; Stavins, 2008), learning-by-doing, innovation spillover effects, and peer effects in the PV industry(Arrow, 1962; Gillingham and Sweeney, 2012; McDonald and Schrattenholzer, 2001; van Benthem et al., 2008; Verdolini and Galeotti, 2011).

① Wind emits even less than solar PV, and the number is 26 tons of CO_2e per GWh.

Other factors driving policy decisions to support solar include the potential benefits of energy resource diversity(i.e. energy security) and the potential of new jobs and increased economic activity in the solar sector(Fischer and Preonas, 2010). In addition, since most of the incentive programs affect the demand side, the induced innovation engendered by these demand-pull policies brings in additional benefits to society(Hickes, 1932; Jaffe and Newell, 2002; Lanzi and Sue Wing, 2011; Nemet, 2009a; Popp et al., 2010). As solar deployment increases rapidly due to these demand-pull policies, solar modules, the key component of a PV system, have experienced a cost reduction by a factor of over 100 since the 1950s(Maycock, 2002; Nemet, 2006), with recent prices as low as 60~70 cents per Watt(GTM Research, 2014).

Direct policy instruments that support solar PV deployment can take many forms, including feed-intariffs(FiT), renewable portfolio standards, investment tax credits(ITC), upfront rebates, net metering, favorable financing, mandatory access, and public investment. Indirect policy tools also exist such as carbon tax and cap-and-trade. The relative merits of these instruments have been broadly studied and debated(Fischer and Newell, 2008; Fullerton and Melcalf, 2001; Nordhaus, 1992; Pizer, 1999; Vollebergh and van der Werf, 2014; Weitzman, 1974). While recognizing the complexity of the problem, this dissertation decides to focus on one of the policy tools – the upfront rebates program, though from several different perspectives. The understanding of the design features and effectiveness of this policy tool provides a strong foundation to study inter-policy relationships in the future.

Upfront rebates directly speak to the high capital cost problem facing potential PV adopters, which is one of the major barriers① to the diffusion of renewable energy technologies(Beck and Martinot, 2004; Hoff, 2006; Sawin, 2004; Verbruggen et al., 2010). Though the average PV installation price has come down dramatically in recent years(Barbose et al., 2014), a typical residential PV system in the U.S.

① Other barriers could be social and behavioral, such as risk aversion, lack of trusted information, decision heuristics, and path-dependence, see Kemp and Volpi(2008) for a good review on this topic.

(4kW) still costs around $20,000 on a pre-rebate basis. In the U.S., the upfront rebate only exists at the state level or below,[①] and governments usually base their rebate on PV system production(i.e. performance), capacity, or both. Production-based subsidies encourage better siting, configuration, and operation and maintenance(O&M), thus maximizing potential production by tying the incentives to system performance; whereas capacity-based subsidies address the capital cost problem directly and play a significant role in attracting lower PV capacity customers and small projects(Barbose et al., 2006; Black, 2006; Connor et al., 2009; Hoff, 2006; IPCC, 2011).

For both production-based and capacity-based incentives, setting an appropriate incentive level is always a major challenge for policymakers. Since the PV technology is evolving rapidly, it becomes difficult to set up the incentive at the right level: too high an incentive level would attract too many applications leading to a run on the program's budget, while too low a level would do little to induce market growth. Chapter 3 tackles this problem in the framework of dynamic programming, which has been applied before in the literature to tackle similar problems. I use the biggest state-level rebate program in the Unites States, the California Solar Initiative(CSI), as the central example for its empirical focus. The availability of rich data for CSI and its significant scale offer a good opportunity to examine the problem in detail. While Chapter 2 introduces the CSI policy, Chapter 3 provides several key insights regarding subsidy policy design focusing on its cost effectiveness.

Another important perspective on the question of subsidy policy design looks at the redistribution effect. This effect is concerned with where the subsidy finally ends up, and whether it benefits consumers or suppliers more. This is an important and much studied question in public economics, i.e. the so-called subsidy incidence or incentive pass-through question. However, despite CSI's significant

---

① The U.S. federal government currently offers 30% investment tax credits to both residential and commercial solar systems, which also has an upfront nature. Nonetheless, the lack of policy variation is not suitable to parameterization in either the dynamic programming modeling or the incentive pass-through analyses.

program budget(over $2 billion), there are few studies that carefully study at the incentive pass-through question for CSI.① Chapter 4 fills in the gap and adopts two approaches to answer this question: structural modeling based on the conduct parameter approach and a reduced-form regression analysis. In my analysis I view these two approaches as being complementary to each other, since different underlying assumptions and data requirements are involved.

In Chapter 5 I employ an as-if natural experiment design to re-examine the incentive pass-through question using a regression discontinuity(RD) design. Under certain assumptions, the RD design could improve the internal validity of research similar to randomized control experiments(Imbens and Lemieux 2008; Lee, 2008). That is one of major reasons for the increasing popularity and adoption of this method in economics and other areas in the social sciences. As for CSI, the pre-determined incentive level stepwise changes and the geographic borders between two neighboring utilities provide good opportunities to apply the RD design. As a result, the derived incentive pass-through rate can be claimed as causal effects, a further robustness check to estimates from Chapter 4, while the latter complements Chapter 5 by providing external validity to the pass-through results. The results from these two chapters have direct implications for subsidy policy design. A complete pass-through rate indicates that the subsidy has benefited fully the intended recipient, i.e. the consumers, and that the induced market competition by the subsidy policy is probably high.

Chapter 6 concludes the dissertation, while synthesizing findings from the core Chapters 3~5, upon which the dissertation is centered. It further discusses fruitful research directions as next steps. The conclusion is kept short by choice, since there are corresponding conclusion sections in each of the core chapters. Overall, this dissertation makes both empirical and methodological contributions to the public policy literature, especially in policy design and evaluation. First of all, it serves as a

① In Chapter 4, this dissertation also leverages data from the prior program to CSI in California, the Emerging Renewables Program(ERP). Thus, the estimated pass-through rate is for both programs.

thorough empirical study of incentive policy design, from both a cost-effectiveness perspective(Chapter 3) and a redistribution point of view(Chapter 4 and 5). Second, methodologically Chapter 3 extends the deterministic dynamic programming framework to further incorporate the stochastic learning-by-doing phenomenon. The considerations of various PV demand functional forms and policy flexibility as well as policy certainty are also new to the literature. Third, Chapters 4 and 5 examine the incentive pass-through question from multiple angles, and they are quite comprehensive in looking at this specific problem for solar PV. Lastly, Chapter 5 also develops several adaptions of the RD design to fit the PV price data, as they proved to be important in removing potential biases in the estimation process.

Chapter 2 Policy Introduction: the California Solar Initiative

CSI is the largest state-level incentive program for solar technologies. A total budget of $2,167 million is divided among the general market($1,897 million); two low-income household programs($216.6 million); research, development, and demonstration($50 million); and a solar water pilot program($3 million). In the general market, CSI has a capacity goal of 1,750MW from 2007 to 2016, with separate goals for different customer segments. The residential market accounts for one third of the target(578MW) and the nonresidential market the other 1,173MW. Each of these two segment targets, in turn, is prorated among the three California investor-owned utilities(IOUs) based on their annual revenues, which is also the basis for the CSI budget contribution from these utilities. These three IOUs include Pacific Gas & Electric Company(PG&E), Southern California Edison Company(SCE), and San Diego Gas & Electric(SDG&E)[①].

The system size covered by CSI varies from 1kW to 1MW CEC-AC[②]. While the program is mainly for PV, it also accommodates electric generating solar thermal

① People sometimes refer to California Center for Sustainable Energy(CCSE) instead of SDG&E, because CCSE helps manage the CSI program for SDG&E. I consider them equivalent in this dissertation.

② California Energy Commission Alternating Current is PTC Rating × Number of Modules × Inverter Efficiency(CPUC, 2014).

technologies[①] at a capped budget of $100.8 million, around 5% of the CSI budget. However, this chapter does not include non-PV technologies since their technology characteristics and development are different. The focus of this dissertation is PV in the general market in California. Sometimes, only data from the residential segment is used for reasons explained later.

Next, I am going to highlight the first important document on CSI, the joint staff report, then introduce the incentive adjustment mechanism adopted by CSI to motivate my cost-effectiveness analysis, and finally discuss the CSI incentive application process to motivate my redistribution analysis.

1)The Joint Staff Report

The idea of CSI stemmed from former Governor Schwarzenegger's Million Solar Roofs Program in August 2004(R0403017[②]). To fulfill this program's target, the California Public Utilities Commission(CPUC) and California Energy Commission(CEC) drafted a joint staff report in June 2005 proposing to consolidate two existing programs—the Emerging Renewables Program(ERP) for residential systems, and the Self-Generation Incentive Program(SGIP) for systems of at least 30kW(mainly commercial systems)—into a new CSI. The aim is to create a "one-stop-solar-shop".

As stated clearly in the joint staff report, the objectives of the program are to(R0403017, p.4):

- Add clean, distributed contribution to our peak demand resources.
- Reduce risk by diversifying California's energy portfolio.
- Lower the burden of expanding and maintaining the State's transmission,

① These solar thermal technologies mainly include electric displacing solar thermal(generally defined as solar forced air heating and solar cooler or air conditioning) and electric generating solar thermal(generally defined as dish Stirling, solar trough and concentrating solar technologies). Notice that these technologies do not include solar water heating. Anyway, only electric generating solar thermal technologies receive CSI rebates.

② Hereafter, notations such as R0403017 and D0601024 refer to the official ruling and decision documents made by the California Public Utilities Commission(CPUC).

pipeline, and distribution systems for electricity and natural gas.

• Demonstrate a long-term commitment to solar energy.

• Establish a program plan under which solar products and providers can transition to a market without incentives.

• Include protocols to allow residents of affordable housing to utilize solar technologies they might not otherwise be able to access.

Furthermore, the report mentioned that this program would contribute "to significantly increase the amount of renewable generation and distributed generation in California and thereby decrease GHG emissions, improve air quality, and diversify California's energy portfolio". It seems that environmental benefits only come as a second-order effect. This will influence the model setup in Chapter 3, especially in terms of model objective selection.

After deciding what the program goal(s) is, the natural next step is policy design, i.e. how to provide what kind of incentives and to whom? A couple of relevant policy design elements are important: • What is the appropriate system eligibility: system size measurement, size range, technology types, and energy efficiency requirement? • Whether to design different programs for different segments or to collapse them into one? • Whether to provide a capacity-based incentive or a production-based one or both? • Should the incentive differ among different customer segments? • How to adjust the incentive level over time? • How to expand this program to benefit low-income people? Although all of them are important, the fifth element is most interesting and discussed the most in the joint report and later documents. From an optimization perspective, this element is the only one that has a time dimension. On the other hand, when looking at similar program experiences from Japan, Germany and Spain, the biggest lesson is to avoid abrupt changes in the policy that "created high demand for PV systems in a very short period, leading to the current supply and demand imbalance"(R0403017, p.5), as happened in both Germany and Spain. Such a concern had driven the joint staff to "Develop a predictable automatic trigger-mechanism to minimize short-term funding gaps, ensure long-term funding availability, and optimize ratepayer funds spent on solar installations"(R0403017, p.11).

2)Megawatt–Triggering Mechanism

Beginning with the idea that the incentives should decline over the program period, it was initially envisaged that CSI would start with a combination of two automatic-reduction mechanisms for adjusting rebate levels over time. The upfront rebate(Expected Performance Based Buydown, namely EPBB) level started at $2.5/W in 2007 and was automatically reduced by 10% per year, i.e., $0.25/W. Moreover, an even faster trigger for rebate reduction would occur when the annual capacity target is achieved early. Under this proposal, the final rebate reduction would depend on which one is triggered first. As specified in a later CPUC proceeding file(R0603004), the 10% standard was considered because of its simplicity and transparency, especially when it was very difficult to set the "ideal" rebate level.①

In a later decision(D0608028), the 10% automatic reduction was discarded and CPUC adopted a mechanism solely based on a megawatt-triggering system. This was called the new adjustment mechanism—a "waterfall" style trigger, since once the megawatt target at each step is completed, the incentive level automatically drops to the next level. Thus, the megawatt step is not linked to the calendar year any more. Depending on market forces, the annual budget could be exhausted—and the annual capacity installed—more quickly or more slowly than "scheduled". The reason behind this design(which became the final version) is its flexibility. As indicated in the decision, the 10% reduction per year risked stalling California's solar market, because if system prices failed to drop by the same amount(10%), installing

① CPUC actually considered four alternatives before arriving at this decision: 1)increased monitoring of market factors that impact installed system costs, e.g., module price and actual system performance; 2)a flexible quarterly market trigger based on whether the budget is constrained or not; 3)an economic model accounting for various market variables and seeking optimum incentive levels; and 4)an auction design. All of these alternatives were rejected for different reasons.

solar systems would become less attractive①, and installers would move to other more lucrative markets. On the other hand, the megawatt-triggering mechanism could reflect the economics of the solar market without employing any economic formula or review process.

The megawatt-triggering system can be summarized in Figure 1. Within each of the three largest electric utility service territories in California, the rebate level decreased stepwise once a certain capacity goal for each step had been achieved. The starting rebate level is \$2.5/W, and the final rebate level is \$0.2/W, after which the program ends. Overall, the CSI sets up nine steps for the whole process. At the beginning of the CSI in early 2007, a typical residential PV system could receive an upfront rebate of \$2.5/W based on system size(and scaled by the expected performance of the system), whereas the system installation price was on average around \$10/W.② In Figure 1, the X-axis denotes the nine steps, from Step 2 to 10, for the major incentive type available to the residential sector: Expected Performance Based Buydown(EPBB).③ For each step, the CSI established a capacity goal and a corresponding rebate level. The steps move to the next level once the stepwise capacity goal is achieved.

The three IOUs in California administer this rebate program in their own territories with different capacity goals, and they have generally moved at different paces along the rebate ladders. Table 1 further breaks the capacity target down by IOUs and by customer segments. The ratio of capacity goals allocated among PG&E, SCE, and SDG&E, which was based on the number of customers in each utility area, is 1 : 1.05 : 0.24. However, it does not imply that these three IOUs will have the same PV adoption speed over time. On the other hand, the

① This argument is based on the untested assumption of a complete(100%) pass-through rate of the rebate. Complete pass-through means that for the same price of PV installation, if the rebate level decreases by 10%, then the net price paid by consumers will *increase* by 10%. Additional ongoing work by the authors examines this question in more detail.

② Prior to the CSI, the ERP at times offered even higher rebate levels.

③ The other type is the Performance-Based Incentive(PBI), which accounts for less than 0.5% of the residential systems; the present study only covers EPBB.

ratio of capacity goals between residential and non-residential segments is roughly 1 : 2, while the latter is a combination of commercial, governmental, and NGOs. Furthermore, CSI regulates that commercial systems will receive the same rebate level as residential ones, while the GOV/NGO systems will receive a higher rebate① level to reflect their inability to explore the tax credit benefits available at the state or federal levels.

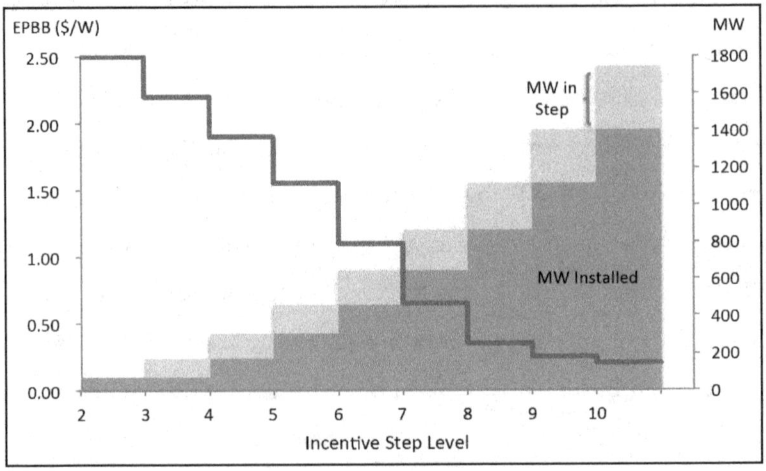

Figure 1 CSI EPBB Capacity Steps and Rebate Levels

Table 1 CSI Capacity Targets by IOUs and Customer Segments

		PG&E(MW)		SCE(MW)		SDG&E(MW)	
Step	MW in Step	Res	Non-Res	Res	Non-Res	Res	Non-Res
1	50	—	—	—	—	—	—
2	70	10.1	20.5	10.6	21.6	2.4	4.8
3	100	14.4	29.3	15.2	30.8	3.4	6.9
4	130	18.7	38.1	19.7	40.1	4.4	9.0
5	160	23.1	46.8	24.3	49.3	5.4	11.0
6	190	27.4	55.6	28.8	58.6	6.5	13.1

① Hereafter, this dissertation uses terms of incentive, rebate, and subsidy interchangeably.

Continuation

		PG&E(MW)		SCE(MW)		SDG&E(MW)	
Step	MW in Step	Res	Non-Res	Res	Non-Res	Res	Non-Res
7	215	31.0	62.9	32.6	66.3	7.3	14.8
8	250	36.1	73.2	38.0	77.1	8.5	17.3
9	285	41.1	83.4	43.3	87.8	9.7	19.7
10	350	50.5	102.5	53.1	107.9	11.9	24.2
Total	1750	252.4	512.3	265.6	539.5	59.5	120.8
Total by Utility		764.8		805.0		180.3	
Percent		43.7%		46.0%		10.3%	

Source: CPUC, 2014.

To sum up, the CSI MW triggering mechanism sets up an automatic incentive adjustment process, which reduces the incentive level over time in steps, reflecting the expectation that the technology cost will go down in the future. This mechanism also differentiates utility service territories in response to their varying demand conditions, and provides different incentive levels to different customer segments.

3)Incentive Application Process

The CSI incentive application process consists of three major steps: incentive reservation, system installation, and incentive claim. All stages involve a solar PV installer, also known as a solar contractor. Typically, the installer will look at customers' rooftop situation, get the most productive solar system, provide the quote, help apply for the CSI incentive(i.e. incentive reservation), install the system, seek various permits, and finally help claim the incentive. In practice, though PV customers could apply for the incentives directly, the vast majority instead authorizes PV installers to submit incentive claims on their behalf; the PV installers then provide PV customers a discount on the installation prices that is equal to the incentive received.

Information on the then-current rebate level and the remaining capacity goals before the step changes has been constantly updated at csi-trigger.com for each IOU and each customer segment. Also, another website(californiasolarstatistics.ca.gov) provides easily downloadable dataset to the public on all the systems CSI funded in the past, including their information on system size(and other system characteristics), installed price, rebate received, key incentive application process dates, utilities, customer segment, installer, zip code, city and county. Such policy transparency allows both customers and installers to understand better what their peers have done, and what their expectations should be.

Since the CSI incentive is decreasing over time, one of the most important considerations customers have is to obtain as a high incentive level as possible. As a result, the portion paid out of their pockets will be lower. On the other hand, another countervailing factor to consider is postponed buying, which allows customers to explore the option value to wait and potentially enjoy the lower costs in the future. These two factors will potentially confound any research attempts to model PV demand, since they create the so-called selection bias problems. In other words, different customers at different adoption time tend to have different price elasticities and discount factors; research designs should take these customer heterogeneities and their distribution over time into account.

One way to exhibit the selection bias is in Figure 2, which shows the daily application numbers based on the incentive reservation review date for the PG&E residential segment. This date has been used by IOUs(as the CSI program administrators) to determine which rebate step/level they are going to assign each application to. Based on Figure 2, right before the date that the rebate level decreases(I call it the stepdown date thereafter), as indicated by the red vertical lines, many more people will apply for the CSI rebate in PG&E. Similarly things happen in other utilities, too. This clearly shows that people self-select to be on the left side of the stepdown date, maybe because of their own information or because of installers' special marketing activities. People have characterized this rushing-up phenomenon as the "Announcement Effect"(Gürtler and Sieg, 2010) or the "pulling-forward effect"(Rogers, 2014).

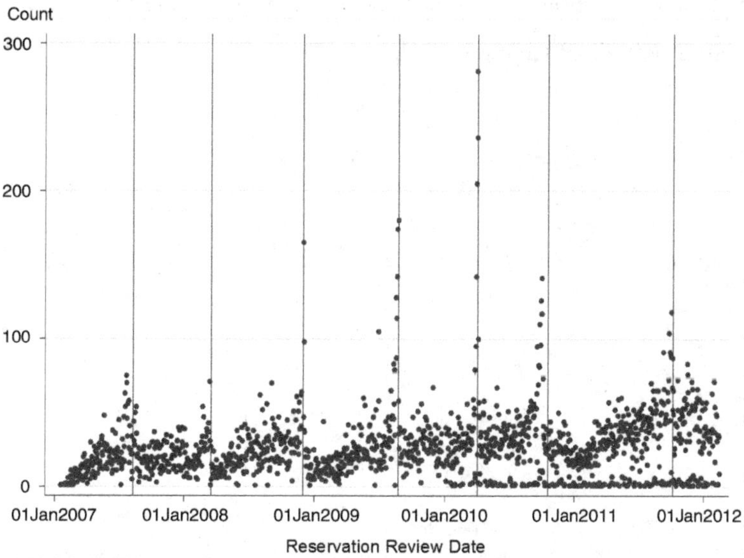

Figure 2 Daily Incentive Application Numbers in the PG&E Residential Segment

What the "Announcement Effect" does is shifting demand around from post-stepdown period(say Period Ⅱ) to pre-stepdown period(say Period Ⅰ). This will deflate the quantity change in reaction to any price variation within these two periods, resulting in a flatter demand curve(or a less negative price coefficient). Such a issue is most serious if estimating a demand equation using daily installation data, as shown in Figure 2. However, using longer period averages should be able to alleviate the problem. In Chapter 3, I use quarterly data to estimate the demand equation, which has similar results to the case using annual data. Secondly, using net price(i.e. price minus incentive) information rather than the price variable in the demand equation will also make the change in the independent variable bigger; since the change in the dependent variable(i.e. quantity) and the change in the independent variable(i.e. net price) usually take different signs, the deflation in the former and the inflation in the latter will counteract each other, resulting in a smaller bias. In Chapter 3, I used net price rather than price in the demand equation. Lastly, if there were no price change before and after the stepdown date, the problem disappears in the demand equation estimation, since any change in the quantity should be attributed to other reasons than price. That is what I find in the redistribution analysis of Chapters 3~4.①

① Imagine the price, incentive and quantity before the stepdown is p_0, r_0 and q_0, after the stepdown, they become p_1, r_1 and q_1. For CSI, by definition, $r_1<r_0$. Using price in the demand equation, the demand slope is $\rho_1=\frac{q_1-q_0}{p_1-p_0}$. What the "Announcement Effect" does is to shift $\Delta q(>0)$ demand from q_1 to q_0. Now the demand slope becomes $\rho_2=\frac{q_1-q_0-2\Delta q}{p_1-p_0}$, i.e. the change in quantity is deflated. If using net price in the demand equation, the demand slope is $\rho_3=\frac{q_1-q_0-2\Delta q}{p_1-p_0+(r_0-r_1)}$, i.e. the change in price is inflated. Obviously, ρ_3 is closer to ρ_1 than ρ_2 to ρ_1. On the other hand, if $p_1=p_0$, there is no price change before and after the stepdown, and then, the demand slope will be zero if just focusing on the no-price-change window. As a result, there would be no bias in the demand equation estimation.

Chapter 3 Optimal Subsidy Design with Stochastic Learning: A Dynamic Programming Evaluation of the California Solar Initiative

1)Introduction

Market failures such as unpriced environmental consequences of conventional energy sources(Baumol and Oates, 1988; Bezdek, 1993; Painuly, 2002; Stavins, 2008), learning-by-doing, innovation spillover effects, and peer effects(Arrow, 1962; McDonald and Schrattenholzer, 2001; van Benthem et al., 2008; Verdolini and Galeotti, 2011) are commonly associated with the adoption of renewable energy technologies and energy conservation measures(Gillingham and Sweeney, 2012; Jaffe et al., 2005; Levine et al., 1995). To address these market failures, there exist various forms of subsidies for renewable technology adoption(Azuela & Barroso, 2011; Bird et al., 2012; Fischer &Preonas, 2010; REN21, 2013). For example, for the adoption of solar photovoltaic(PV), aside from tax credits and loan options, governments usually subsidize PV based on production(i.e. performance), capacity, or both. Production-based subsidies encourage better siting, configuration, and operation and maintenance(O&M), thus maximizing potential production by tying the incentives to system performance; whereas capacity-based subsidies address the capital problem directly and play a significant role in attracting small customers and small projects(Barbose et al., 2006; Black, 2006; Connor et al., 2009; Hoff, 2006; IPCC, 2011).

For both production-based and capacity-based incentives, setting an appropriate incentive level is always a major challenge for policymakers. There are many examples in PV of setting the incentive levels too high[①] and attracting too many subscriptions, including in Britain(Vaughan et al., 2011), Australia(Macintosh and Wilkinson, 2011), and several state-level programs in the United States(Bird et al., 2012). Further, because policy certainty and predictability are important to industry stakeholders(Couture, 2009; IEA, 2008; Klein et al., 2008; Mendonça, 2007; Sawin, 2004), incentive levels need to be set in advance and adjusted in a predictable way that affords continuity. However, not knowing the future technology costs and demand levels makes this task challenging(Bird et al., 2012).

The relevant literature on optimal energy subsidy dates back to Baumol and Bradford(1970), Schmalensee(1980), and Solomon and Georgianna(1987). These papers looked at the subsidy problem from an all-encompassing perspective on energy sources. While focusing on a specific energy sector, Vedenov and Wetzstein(2008) extended the framework developed by Parry and Small(2005) and looked at the optimal subsidy for ethanol fuel, whereas Wu et al.(2012) examined the socially optimal biodiesel subsidy for the United States. However, these studies relied on comparative statics and tended to neglect the importance of learning-by-doing effects and peer effects[②], which may significantly impact the supply and demand functions, respectively.

In the marketing literature, researchers have looked at the optimal subsidy problem from a different angle. Of particular relevance is the Bass diffusion model,

---

① This is only too high from a program management perspective, i.e. the subsidy level is too high if it attracts too many subscriptions and the program budget runs out quicker than expected. Nonetheless, this does not mean the subsidy level is too high from a broad social welfare perspective.

② I use peer effects and penetration effects interchangeably in this chapter. Strictly speaking, the latter would include other effects of existing cumulative capacity on current period demand than just peer effects. I use these terms in this broader sense.

which incorporates word-of-mouth and learning-by-doing(LBD) effects into the demand function(Kalish and Lilien, 1983; Peng, 2013; Zaccour, 1996). The major conclusion is that, whenever the word-of-mouth effect(also called peer effect) is high, the optimal subsidy should be monotonically decreasing. Since a significant peer effect exists for solar PV(Bollinger and Gillingham, 2012; Rai and Robinson, 2013), any model of optimal solar subsidy should be dynamic and include this effect. That is why increasingly researchers are employing Dynamic programming(DP) techniques for calculating optimal PV subsidies.

Within the DP framework, van Benthem et al.(2008) studied the California Solar Initiative(CSI), and later research has tended to focus on the feed-in-tariff(FIT) policy in Germany(Creti and Joaug, 2012; Lobel and Perakis, 2011; Wand and Leuthold, 2011). van Benthem et al.(2008) bundled a logistic demand curve with a LBD type of technological change and found that CSI is very close to being socially optimal when considering environmental externalities. However, the CSI subsidy schedule(10% annual deduction) used by van Benthem et al.(2008) is not exactly the one that was finally implemented(see Section 3.2 for more details). Further, they assumed the state tax credit to last through 2016, but it actually ended in 2005. If these modifications were accounted for, then their results would point to a higher-than-CSI subsidy policy from a socially optimal perspective. Wand and Leuthold(2011) applied a very similar model to the German FIT. These two studies did not model peer effects directly. Creti and Joaug(2012) adopted a(binary) discrete choice model and LBD developed by Lobel and Perakis(2011) to model the FIT more directly($/kWh), while the latter instead modeled the optimal upfront rebate for Germany($/kWp). Alizamir et al.(2012) developed a similar DP model for FIT with endogenous policy horizon, but no data analysis or simulation was implemented.

A missing piece from the above DP work is the role of market uncertainties. The PV industry is exposed to the vagaries of the silicon supply chain and other demand conditions. The uncertainty with respect to LBD is addressed by several empirical(reduced-form) analyses(Nemet, 2009b; van der Zwaan and Rabl, 2004), but it has not been sufficiently addressed by more structured models. One exception is the research on the uncertainty of investment decisions(Bloom, 2009; Bloom et al., 2007; Dixit and Pindyck, 1994; Pindyck, 2012). Fertig and Apt(2012) applied this method to the optimal R&D strategy for PV, whereas Bauner and Crago(2013) extended the work of Ansar and Sparks(2009) to study the effect of uncertainties on the household's decision to adopt PV. However, the latter two studies focused on the option value only, and do not address the optimal subsidy question. Overall, the implication after bringing in uncertainties to either the cost drift function or the payoff function—similar to the case when a positive option value exists—is that uncertainties are found to require higher subsidies than in the deterministic case(Cohen et al., 2013).

This chapter recognizes the challenges of designing a suitable subsidy policy for incentivizing the adoption of renewable energy technologies amidst volatile demand, technology shocks on product costs, and need for policy flexibility and certainty. Accordingly, I focus on the CSI policy case and aim to find the optimal subsidy schedule with hindsight, with due consideration to inherent supply-side learning stochasticity. I would like to note that in this chapter by optimal subsidy I am referring to the cost-effectiveness of a policy rather than its broader social optimality. This is in keeping with most solar subsidy programs, including CSI, where governments offer solar-specific subsidies to address market failures such as peer effects and learning-by-doing that may be particularly pronounced in the sector. For solar-specific subsidy programs, then the focus clearly shifts to setting of the rebate schedule so as to maximize the total installed PV capacity when subject to a pre-defined budget constraint. That is the question I study in this chapter.

Besides its high significance within the United States, CSI is a good choice for the analysis because of the excellent availability of data and of its transparent policy context. Although CSI is mainly based on an upfront subsidy, its similarity with performance-based incentives(PBI) in an optimized framework is high. Once a FIT is guaranteed(say for 20 years) and kept constant, it can be regarded as upfront after discounting and assuming an average electricity generation value, as done in Lobel and Perakis(2011).

The rest of the chapter is organized as follows. Section 3.2 describes the CSI policy history and design process, which is important for building the optimization model later on. Section 3.3 introduces the DP model to capture the essence of the optimal PV subsidy problem, and the parameterization process. In Section 3.4, the DP model is first solved analytically and then computationally in both deterministic and stochastic cases, where the latter is characterized by incorporating stochastic LBD into the DP framework. Finally, Section 3.5 provides conclusions and insights for policy design.

2)The California Solar Initiative: Policy in Retrospect

The following subsections address how CSI arrived at its capacity targets and budget, how CSI determined its incentive level for each step within the MW-triggering mechanism, and how CSI has performed in terms of achieving its capacity targets.

(1)CSI Target and Budget Setting

The joint staff report drew on experiences from previous programs in California and other countries, and it proposed a \$1.1 billion~\$1.8 billion plan to achieve a 3,000MW capacity goal. However, comments received suggested that both these initial capacity targets and budgets were unrealistic(R0403017, Appendix A). A revised version of CSI(D0601024) increased the budget to \$2.8 billion for the same target of 3,000MW from 2007 to 2016, including a CPUC portion of \$2.5 billion and 2,600MW.① Meanwhile, a capacity target for each year was established for the first time with a corresponding incentive level(i.e. incentive step).

In August 2006, SB 1 cut the CPUC portion of the program to \$2.16 billion, to be distributed among the three major IOUs. As a result, CPUC decided(D0612033) to assume only the budget-proportional part of the 3,000MW target: 1,940MW, or 65% of the target(\$2.16 billion/\$3.35 billion). 90% of the budget and target(1,750MW) were assigned to the mainstream incentive program.② The annual

① The remainder of the budget and capacity target were allocated to CEC management.

② The remaining 10% was for low-income household programs. Later, the mainstream incentive program in D1009046 was changed, which is not important for the present discussion.

capacity targets were then reduced after year five, according to this new overall target. This brief note on CSI's background suggests that budget should be a rigid constraint rather than an objective, as is the case in cost minimization DP models.

(2)Megawatt–Triggering Mechanism

After choosing the triggering mechanism as the incentive adjustment mechanism, the CPUC staff established the maximum incentive levels for each step using the following four principles(D0608028, p.104~105):

• Incentive drops no more than $0.45 and no less than $0.05;

• Incentive drops of no more than $0.30 in the first two steps(to avoid disruption early on);

• $0.20 per watt to be the minimum meaningful incentive to offer during the last step to close out the program($0.7/W for the government/non-profit sector);

• The government/non-profit sector starts with a higher incentive(SB 1 sets it to be $0.75/W higher), thus a larger drop in the incentive rate for this sector in Steps 9~10 to arrive at a comparable low level with residential and commercial sectors.

• With these rules, the CSI incentive levels were considered "optimized"(D0608028). Table 2 shows the final incentive levels($/W) for each step and each customer segment, which is obviously different from the 10% reduction per year mechanism. Note that the residential and commercial segments share the same rebate schedule.

Table 2 CSI Final Decision on Step-wise Incentive Levels($/W)

Step	MW	Gov/NP – 20%	Res – 33%	Com – 47%[b]	Budget(million)
1	50	n/a	n/a	n/a	n/a
2	70	$3.25	$2.50	$2.50	$186
3	100	$2.95	$2.20	$2.20	$235
4	130	$2.65	$1.90	$1.90	$267
5	160	$2.30	$1.55	$1.55	$272

Continuation

Step	MW	Gov/NP – 20%	Res – 33%	Com – 47%[b]	Budget(million)
6	190	$1.85	$1.10	$1.10	$238
7	215	$1.40	$0.65	$0.65	$172
8	250	$1.10	$0.35	$0.35	$125
9	285	$0.90	$0.25	$0.25	$108
10	350	$0.70	$0.20	$0.20	$105
Target	1,800			Total	$1,708

a. This table is based on Table 3 in Appendix B of D0612033.

b. The three percentages in the title row are the designated proportion of the megawatt target in each sector.

c. This does not include the megawatt target of Step 1.

However, by exploring this assertion using the four CSI principles described above in the Excel Solver, I find that the final rebate schedule is neither unique nor optimal(see more details in Appendix A). For example, CSI requires that the incentive drop in the first two steps be no more than $0.30, but it also seeks to find the maximum incentive for each step with each drop more than $0.05. Therefore, Step 3 could take any value from $2.2 to $2.45, and Step 4 from $1.9 to $2.4, assuming Step 2 is at $2.5/W. Obviously, more constraints need to be imposed to arrive at the final rebate schedule as in CSI(see Appendix A).

(3)CSI Performance

When examining the real performance below, this chapter uses the up-to-date CSI data, but as an illustration in this section I focus only on the EPBB incentive for the residential sector within the Pacific Gas & Electric(PG&E) area. Other sectors in various areas with different types of incentives are very similar.

So how well did CSI achieve its capacity target and adhere to its incentive steps and timeline? Figure 3 shows the capacity target and cumulative installation at each step as well as the promulgated and actual rebate levels, starting from Step 2. For both capacity and rebate, the actual performance is very well aligned with the targets at each step, especially for the rebate levels. Note that this is by design. Furthermore, on the average each step takes roughly three quarters to fulfill the capacity target. As a consequence, the program came to an end in early 2013 for the PG&E service area. In terms of achieving the capacity target, CSI has performed well, reaching final goals three years sooner than originally envisioned. However, after employing the Megawatt-triggering mechanism, there is near certainty for the program in terms of fulfilling its target within the predetermined budget limit. The only real uncertainty is how fast the program moves through its steps and when the program ends. Nevertheless, the real question is how optimal the subsidy policy is and whether the same amount of resources could potentially have led to more PV deployment under a somewhat different program design.

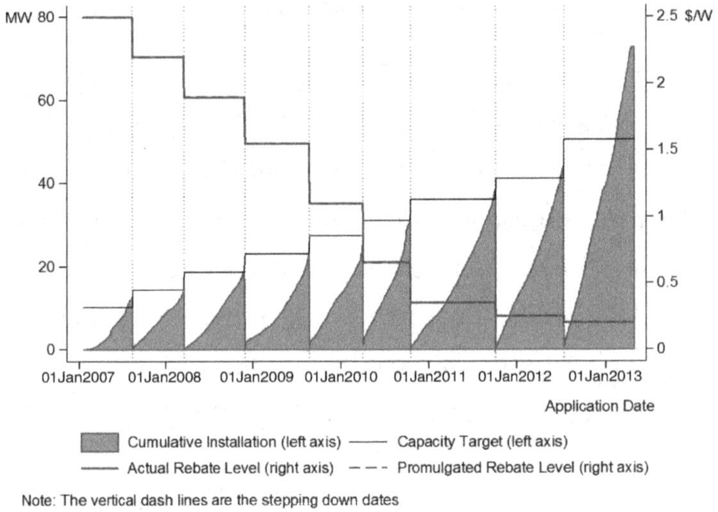

Figure 3 CSI EPBB Performance for Residential Systems in PG&E Service Territory

Note that the capacity-related variables are on the left vertical axis, whereas the rebate-related variables are on the right vertical axis. The vertical dashed lines designate the actual cut-off dates for each step down.

The question then comes down to whether one can change the rebate-level schedule to arrive at the achieved installed capacity or even better results. Also, although CSI stipulates broad constraints linking rebate steps to installed capacity, explicit relationships governing how exactly the rebate levels respond to changes in installed capacity are missing. These issues need to be addressed using an integrated and consistent framework.

3)Modeling and Parameterization

As discussed above, CSI does not appear to have adhered to a robust economic modeling framework—indeed, CSI planning documents appear to reject such an approach(R0603004)—yet it met its capacity target within only six years. CSI is generally considered by analysts to be quite successful. But to really assess the effectiveness of CSI, a PV demand model is needed to control for various contemporaneous factors. That could help answer the following questions: 1)How responsive are consumers to the subsidy and net price changes? 2)What is the impact of other drivers, such as penetration effects and expected electricity price increases, that might exist in the market? As explained below, proceeding to systematically answering these questions is a key piece to the DP model.

In the following, I first present the DP model and discuss some functional-form issues, and then move to the parameterization process for each equation in the DP model. In Section 3.4, I solve the DP model first analytically and then computationally for both deterministic and stochastic cases.

(1)Model Setup

I generally follow similar application of the DP technique in the literature(Creti and Joaug, 2012; Lobel and Perakis, 2011; van Benthem et al., 2008), albeit with a different model setup and estimation process. Our DP model can be summarized as follows(also see Figure 4):

Objective: $$\max_{\{r_t\}} \Sigma_{t=1}^{T} \delta^t q(r)_t \tag{1}$$

Cumulative quantity: $$Q_t = Q_{t-1} + q_t \tag{2}$$

Demand equation: $$q_t = \beta_0 + \beta_1 Q_{t-1} + \beta_2 (p_t - r_t) + \beta_3 E_t + \varepsilon_t \tag{3}$$

Learning-by-doing: $$log(p_t) = log(p_0) + b log(Q_{t-1}) + \omega_t \tag{4}$$

Budget constraint: $$B_t = B_{t-1} - r_t q_t \tag{5}$$

Electricity price: $$E_t = (1 + \rho)\, E_{t-1} \quad (6)$$

The objective function(1) is to maximize the discounted total installation of PV(kW) over a time horizon T with the policy/decision variable r_t as the upfront rebate level(\$/W) at time t. δ is the government discount coefficient, and q_t is the annual installed capacity(kW). The first constraint(2) is straightforward as the definition of cumulative PV capacity, while the second constraint(3) specifies the demand function in a reduced form. The diffusion process(demand function) of q_t is a function of the past cumulative installation level Q_{t-1}, net prices paid by consumers$(p_t - r_t)$(\$/W), electricity price E_t(\$/kWh), and a random shock variable ε_t. The third constraint(4) is a typical LBD equation, where price change(the ratio between the current price level(\$/W) and the initial price level p_0(\$/W)) is determined by the past cumulative capacity installed(Arrow, 1962). The fourth constraint(5) is the budget B_t(\$) appropriated by the subsidy program. Lastly, following the literature(Wand and Leuthold, 2011), the electricity price(\$/kWh) is assumed to be linearly increasing over time with a constant growth rate ρ(6). All constraints(2)~(6) are to be parameterized below, whereas the initial conditions(Q_0, p_0, B_0, E_0) are assumed to be known, and(ε, ω) are random shocks to the system.

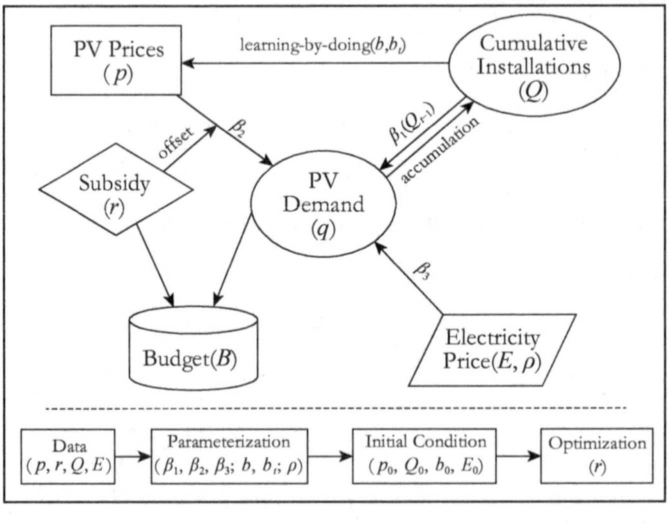

Figure 4 DP Model Process Flow Diagram: Model, Data and Parameterization

The parameterization process for the DP model proceeds as follows(Figure 4): I first estimate the LBD equation(Section 3.3.2.1), since there is only one parameter involved(b); I then compare several different demand model specifications and choose the baseline model(Section 3.3.2.2); and lastly, I consider issues related to the electricity price and the ITC(Section 3.3.2.3). I perform various robustness checks for the model specifications and the parameter estimates. As it turns out in the sensitivity analysis, varying the key parameters in the DP model does not change the central findings.① Overall, these parameterizations allow for an ex post② calculation of the coefficients included in constraint(3) and constraint(4) of the DP model. As a result, the DP model can then be solved(Section 3.4).

Several items require further explanation for the DP model. Firstly, regarding the objective function, the literature chooses to maximize the cumulative diffusion under a budget constraint as this chapter does(Kalish and Lilien, 1983) or the net social benefits(van Benthem et al., 2008), or minimizes the program costs when achieving a certain capacity target(Lobel and Perakis, 2011). While the first and third targets should be dual problems, as discussed in Section 3.2.1, the history of CSI policy-making indicates that the budget should be a more realistic constraint than the capacity target since the target was adapted after the budget changes. In terms of net social benefits, CSI left this problem for later program evaluation(E3, 2011). Therefore, it is reasonable to take the cumulative capacity as the objective, subject to a budget constraint.

Secondly, as to the policy variable, r_t, this chapter focuses on the CSI EPBB part, which is the default incentive form for residential systems.③ The role of default

---

① A related point to note is that it may be possible to estimate some of the parameters(especially LBD) more accurately by bringing additional, disaggregated data to bear. For example, drawing insights and controls from a dynamic oligopoly model of contractor pricing, Bollinger and Gillingham(2013) estimate a reduced-form model of soft costs, yielding robust estimates of LBD. Such a detailed estimation process is not necessary in my study given that the DP model is not significantly sensitive to changes in the value of the key parameters, including LBD.

② The parameterization is *ex post* because it benefits from hindsight—I use the realized market data(demand, prices) over time to estimate the parameters.

③ Studying optimal EPBB can speak directly to the optimal PBI problem, since both can be converted to each other under certain CSI assumptions.

rules has been analyzed substantially in the behavioral economics literature(Beshears et al., 2008; Carlsson and Johansson-Stenman, 2012), and this also applies to CSI applicants, where 99.6% of all residential customers have chosen EPBB instead of PBI even though systems under 30kW have the option to choose PBI.

Finally, the third constraint(4) is typical within the LBD literature, although sometimes researchers(e.g. van Benthem et al., 2008; Wand and Leuthold, 2011) differentiate the LBD for solar panels and for the balance-of-system(BOS). This chapter combines solar panels and BOS together because when introducing dynamic LBD by varying the learning coefficient, it becomes advantageous to deal with one uncertain multiplicative parameter instead of two. In addition, the combined LBD function is able to deliver a similar model goodness-of-fit as the one with the two parts separated.

(2)Parameterization

①LBD Equation

Estimating the LBD equation in constraint(4) is straightforward, but the starting point for the price and cumulative quantity series must be considered carefully. Choosing to use data from CSI only or from both CSI and ERP is an important consideration for obtaining the correct learning coefficient. Using data starting from the ERP program is preferable, since that is the beginning of the California PV mass market and technology learning. Nevertheless, if only the CSI data are used, previous LBD that happened under ERP must be accounted for; not doing so will underestimate the learning coefficient. This chapter uses data from both ERP and CSI, extending from 1998 to 2012. All the(pre-incentive) price data are adjusted to 2012 real dollars based on the Consumer Price Index. Note that after I plug the obtained learning coefficient into the DP model, the price term becomes endogenous in the sense that it is totally determined by the model.

The estimated learning coefficient is −0.075, with the t-statistic as −6.48, significant at the 99.9% level. This estimate is very similar whether using annual or quarterly data. As a result, the learning rate is $1-2^{b}=0.05$, implying that for each doubling of cumulative installed capacity, the average PV price in California would fall by 5%. In contrast, van Benthem et al.(2008) used a learning rate of 0.10, with the corresponding learning coefficient of −0.152. This difference is mainly because the studied period in their work ended in 2006. After that period, the PV market experienced much faster and larger growth but lower price reduction except in recent years(Figure 5). van Benthem et al.(2008) did vary the learning rate in their sensitivity analysis; for a learning rate of 0.05(as used in this chapter), the average optimal incentive level in their model drops substantially from nearly \$2/W to around \$0.5/W. This chapter further addresses this issue of different parameter values in the sensitivity analysis presented later.

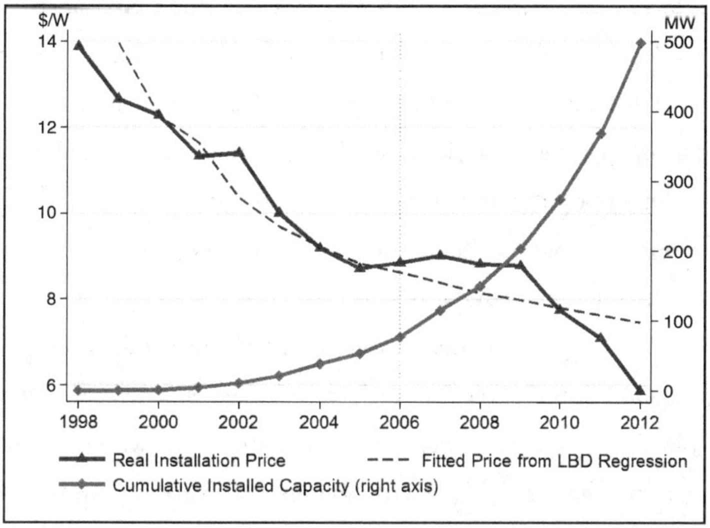

Figure 5 LBD Fit and Comparison between pre-and-post 2006

Also in Figure 5, LBD seems to show some variation or stochasticity during this period, especially after 2006. While the LBD is slower from 2006 to 2009, it picks up its momentum again in 2010. Other research has noted similar heterogeneity in LBD(Citi Research, 2014), and this might suggest that additional reasons, most importantly equipment costs, exist to explain the anomalies in the price trajectories. As discussed below, this chapter models this through a stochastic LBD approach, meaning the learning coefficient is varied over time, which should be sufficient to capture such a trend.

②Demand Equation

The demand equation specification usually involves the greatest divergence of approaches in the literature. There are several different ways to model an S-shaped demand curve: Bass-type diffusion models(Bass, 1969; Bass et al., 1994; Kalish and Lilien, 1983), direct logistic-type models(van Benthem et al., 2008; Wand and Leuthold, 2011) and discrete choice models(Creti and Joaug, 2012; Lobel and Perakis, 2011). While the latter two both utilize the logistic function, the Bass-type diffusion models could be either attributed to word-of-mouth effects or linked to consumer heterogeneity[①] through some distributions(e.g., shifted Gompertz, see Bemmaor, 1994). Interestingly, the discrete choice models end up with the same word-of-mouth term, i.e., past cumulative adoption, in the reduced form, but are derived from a different theoretical background. The difference between these two approaches is that the Bass models are modeling conditional probability of adoption on the non-adopter population, while the others do not.

This chapter adopts the simple demand model as specified in constraint(3), based on model selection standards and data considerations. Before diving into the actual estimation process, the chosen specification needs more justification. First consideration is the choice of using net present value(NPV) versus the net price term(plus other benefit terms). NPV is a compound measure of the financial benefits based on the price, electricity savings, and various forms of subsidies. As the first PV adopters usually face a negative NPV, fitting NPV to adoption is primarily determined by those negative NPV values at the beginning of the sample periods, as can be seen in van Benthem et al.(2008) and Wand and Leuthold(2011) such as environmental externalities and learning-by-doing(LBD). Another problem with NPV is that, by combining several random variables together, the correlation between NPV and the dependent variable(i.e., level of adoption) is reduced, resulting in a lower model goodness-of-fit. Lastly, measurement error could further compound the NPV calculation since there are several benefit and cost items to

---

① Other work that used consumer heterogeneity to construct S demand curves includes Cabral(2005) and Shum(2013).

consider.① Therefore, this chapter uses the direct net price term and other value terms individually rather than NPV. Nevertheless, a comparison is done below to show the difference.

The second consideration is the functional form of the demand equation. While log-linear specifications② are used in some of the literature(Creti and Joaug, 2012; Lobel and Perakis, 2011), this chapter adopts the simple linear form. To support this conclusion, specification tests are carried out subsequently. There may be a log-linear relationship between demand and the price term; however, it does not necessarily apply to the relationship of demand with NPV, as suggested by the data. Furthermore, the linear form can allow us to utilize the quarterly data and easily convert the coefficients back to the yearly version, thus giving more degrees-of-freedom for the regression.

Thirdly, two other variables are used in the following estimation but not included in the final DP model: federal investment tax credits(ITC)(state ITC before 2005) and the number of active installers. The former is assumed constant in the CSI policymaking process, but its variation has definitely influenced PV adoption(see Section 3.3.2.3 for more details). The second variable is necessary to control for the simultaneity problem between the price and the quantity terms in a demand specification; however, CSI assumed away any constraints from the supply side. While the DP framework tries to stay close to the reality of the conditions and information available at the onset of CSI, the coefficients themselves should be estimated based on what has actually transpired over the period, since ours is an ex post evaluation of the CSI. Otherwise, those omitted variables will cause the coefficients in the demand equation to be biased, thereby hurting the subsequent DP model outcomes.

---

① In the NPV calculation of Creti and Joaug(2012), the authors miscalculated the electricity saving item in that they only included the solar insolation term(kWh/m^2/year) but failed to include a term for the space that a solar system takes up(m^2/kW).

② The log-linear specification regresses the logarithm of the dependent variable(quantity in this case)over the level term of the independent variable(price in this case).

The final regression outputs are summarized in Table 3. Note that the variable of active number of installers is not included at this stage, but only later as part of robustness checks. Also, data prior to 2001 are dropped because far fewer systems were installed during that time. Furthermore, the electricity price is expressed in nominal terms, reflecting what installers are marketing with, while the real prices will not reveal as much movement(Figure 6). Table 3 lists five specifications for explaining PV diffusion. From left to right, they are: a linear model with individual separate net price, electricity price, and ITC terms; a corresponding log-linear model with the logged dependent variable; a linear model with a compound NPV variable and its corresponding log-linear model; and an extended Bass model called R-L(Robinson and Lakhani, 1975).①

I first compare the linear form versus the log-linear form, and then compare the use of the individual value terms(system price; electricity price; and ITC) versus the compound NPV term. For the former, MacKinnon-Davidson PE tests of linearity and log-linearity are done, and the t-statistics are shown in the last row of Table 3. The results indicate a linear relationship rather than a log-linear one between the net price(or the NPV) and the dependent variable, by rejecting the null hypothesis as can be seen in column ⓑ(or column ⓓ). For the second comparison, i.e. whether to include the individual value pieces or the compound NPV term②, the model fit is similar based on the adjusted R-squared values shown in columns ⓐ and ⓒ; however, NPV(per watt) has a smaller coefficient than any of the coefficients for net price, electricity price, and ITC. This is consistent with the expectation mentioned above because of the lower correlation of a compound variable like NPV with the dependent variable. Also as indicated before, at most net price levels the calculated NPV is negative, which is consistent with Drury et al.'s(2011) $4.7/

① The R-L model is specified as: $q_t = (\beta_0 + \beta_1 Q_{t-1} + \beta_2 Q^2_{t+1}) \exp(\beta_3 * NetPrice)$.

② NPV(per watt) is calculated for a lifetime of 25 years, accounting for PV performance degradation(0.5% per year), O&M costs(1.5% of the system price per year), and electricity price increase(3.0% per year), in addition to the three major individual value terms. All assumptions are consistent with the PV cash-flow literature(Black, 2006; Drury et al., 2011; Rai and Sigrin, 2013; Wand and Leuthold, 2011).

W cutoff point(for net price) that separates a negative and a positive NPV. The R-L model seems to have a high goodness-of-fit with fewer explanatory variables, but using either the linear model or the R-L model produces very similar results in the DP model. Thus, the R-L model serves as a cross-validation here. Considering these observations and comparisons, I choose the simple linear functional form as the baseline model for later computational purposes(Eq. 3); but I also verify the main results by running the optimization routing using alternative demand models.

Several results from the linear demand model in Table 3 are noteworthy. First, by including the net price term rather than the price term and rebate term together, I am restricting the magnitude of their coefficients to be the same but with opposite signs. This makes economic sense, since what the rebate does is to offset the price at a one-to-one ratio. Second, the magnitude of the rebate coefficient(same for the price coefficient, both are 2279.9) seems to be larger than that of the electricity price(1201.9); that is because the marginal benefit from one unit increase of the electricity price(i.e. one ¢/kWh) is smaller than that from one unit increase of the rebate(i.e. one $/W), and the ratio of these marginal benefits is well consistent with the ratio of these two coefficients. Third, the ITC coefficient(1163.7) is smaller than that of the rebate, indicating the potential difficulties for residential customers to explore the full benefit of the federal tax credits. All these results are interesting by themselves, and further ensure that the linear demand model is meaningful.

Table 3 Regression Outputs for Different PV Demand Specifications

DV: annual capacity (kW)	Linear ⓐ	Log-linear ⓑ	NPV ⓒ	Log-NPV ⓓ	R-L[a] ⓔ
Lagged cumulative capacity	0.067^{***}	0.499^{***}	0.076^{***}	0.569^{***}	0.394^{***}
(kW)[b]	(0.008)	(0.096)	(0.005)	(0.062)	(0.130)
Lagged cumulative capacity^2					−3.36E−07
(kW^2)					(1.88E−07)

Continuation

DV: annual capacity (kW)	Linear ⓐ	Log-linear ⓑ	NPV ⓒ	Log-NPV ⓓ	R-L[a] ⓔ
Net price = Price – Rebate	−2279.9***	−0.197***			−0.204***
($/W)	(600.0)	(0.047)			(0.043)
Electricity Price (¢/kWh)①	1201.9**	0.178*			
	(574.6)	(0.102)			
ITC($/W)	1163.7**	0.198**			
	(530.0)	(0.073)			
NPV per watt ($/W)			984.5*	0.203***	
			(539.0)	(0.054)	
Constant	−167.15	1.998***	3330.1***	2.910***	2733.7**
	(6016.5)	(0.714)	(1031.1)	(0.748)	(1126.1)
N[c]	48	48	48	48	48
R2_a	0.958	0.918	0.952	0.918	0.982
df_m	4	4	2	2	3
T-stats of linearity or log-linearity[d]	1.463	4.699***	0.055	4.08***	

Note: Robust standard errors in parentheses; *p<0.10, **p<0.05, ***p<0.01.

a. R-L stands for Robinson and Lakhani(1975), which is an extended Bass model. Since it is a nonlinear model, the NLS procedure is used in Stata to obtain the coefficients.

b. This term is logged in the Log-linear and Log-NPV models; also, actual annual data are used for this cumulative term, rather than the quarterly data.②

c. The included sample period is from 2001 through 2012 for all models, where quarterly data are used.

d. Based on MacKinnon-Davidson(PE) test.

---

① Electricity bill savings per watt are calculated too, but the results are similar.

② As mentioned before in the text, quarterly data can be used to convert the coefficient obtained from this four times bigger sample to the annual case; however, this does not work for cumulative terms, like cumulative installed capacity here. The reason is that while $Q_{Y2012}=Q_{Y2011}+q_{Y2012Q1}+q_{Y2012Q2}+q_{Y2012Q3}+q_{Y2012Q4}$, it is not equal to $\frac{1}{4}(Q_{Y2012Q1}+Q_{Y2012Q2}+Q_{Y2012Q3}+Q_{Y2012Q4})$, which is $Q_{Y2011}+q_{Y2012Q1}+\frac{3}{4}q_{Y2012Q2}+\frac{2}{4}q_{Y2012Q3}+\frac{1}{4}q_{Y2012Q4}$.

I further run several robustness checks for the linear demand model specification and arrive at the same conclusion regarding the model estimation. Table 4 presents the relevant results. In the second column, the linear demand model is reproduced from Table 3. The third column applies the standard GMM technique to estimate the same model with both the lagged dependent variable and the price term instrumented by three other variables: the double lagged cumulative capacity, the real installation cost per watt by all other states except California in the Tracking The Sun(TTS) dataset(Barbose et al., 2013), and the number of active installers(defined as installers with at least five annual installations). In the last two columns, either forward installation price(p_{t+1}) or the rebate price interaction term($r_t \cdot p_t$) is employed to see if consumers are reacting significantly to any of these factors after controlling for other factors.

Table 4 Robustness Checks for the Linear Demand Model Specification

DV: annual installed capacity(kW)	Linear	GMM[a]	F_Price	Rebate_Price[b]
Lagged cumulative capacity	0.067***	0.068***	0.068***	0.092***c
(kW)	(0.008)	(0.009)	(0.010)	(0.014)
		[1.467]		
Net price = Price − Rebate	−2279.9***	−1529.6**	−2161.2**	
($/W)	(600.0)	(732.5)	(952.9)	
		[.0049]		
Electricity Price(¢/kWh)	1201.9**	867.6	1319.7*	794.6
	(574.6)	(608.4)	(655.5)	(602.657)
ITC($/W)	1163.7**	953.9	1090.3*	34.381
	(530.0)	(757.7)	(564.30	(795.1)
Forward installation price			290.6	
($/W)[d]			(591.5)	
Rebate per Watt($/W)				3339.2
				(2679.8)
Rebate Price Interaction				−180.76

Continuation

DV: annual installed capacity(kW)	Linear	GMM[a]	F_Price	Rebate_Price[b]
				(155.93)
Hansen's J test of over-identification		3.14334*		
N	48	46	47	48
R2_a	0.958	0.952	0.955	0.946
df_m	4	4	5	5

a. The GMM chi-square tests are listed in the brackets below the standard errors.

b. I could not include the price term in this regression because of multicollinearity issues.

c. This coefficient is inflated, because it also picks up the effect from the decreasing price, which is not included in this column.

d. The variable used here is one quarter forward. Other lead-time variations were also tested.

Note: robust standard errors in parentheses; $^{*}p<0.10$, $^{**}p<0.05$, $^{***}p<0.01$.

The results from the GMM tests seem to indicate that the hypothesis that either the lagged cumulative capacity or the net price is exogenous cannot be rejected based on the GMM chi-square tests. If 2SLS is used instead of GMM, the exogeneity of the lagged cumulative capacity can somehow be rejected. In any case, the coefficients for this variable in these cases are very similar, indicating no serious problem. On the other hand, the over-identification test(Hansen's J test) was rejected, further ensuring the validity of the instrument variables.

Based on the last two columns, there are no significant results regarding either the forward price or the rebate interacted with the price. The one-quarter forward price is used in the fourth column and shows up with the expected positive sign, i.e. lower future price will reduce the current demand due to the potential option value; however, this term is statistically insignificant.① On the other hand, the relatively small negative yet insignificant coefficient of the rebate price interaction term

① Using a longer series of forward installation prices can easily produce a(counter-intuitive) negative coefficient, which means lower future installation price is associated with more PV adoption.

suggests that, after keeping the rebate level constant, the same rebate level could possibly bring more adoption when the price is lower; however, this effect did not pass the significance test. The insignificance of this interaction term suggests that the implicit assumption with the log-linear function form in demand that the same net price change could generate more adoption later than earlier when the capacity base is bigger is too strong.

Finally, with the linear demand specification, the predicted installation in 2007 is 2.1 times higher than the actual capacity(as is the case with all other specifications as well). This is because a large number of installations in that year were attributed to the ERP program, due to over subscription problems in 2006. This poses no problem to the estimation, whether this is included as part of the installations in 2006 or 2007.①

To summarize, this section has examined different demand specifications and decided to use the simple linear demand specification for the DP model based on the robustness check. The linear form is flexible to include other variables, makes use of a greater sample size, and can produce results as meaningful as those of other models(e.g., the R-L model).

③Electricity Price and ITC

Electricity price data are available from the U.S. Energy Information Administration(EIA) website and can vary monthly, quarterly, and annually. This chapter uses annual data for the residential sector in California.② Figure 6 shows

① This could be viewed as a measurement error problem in the dependent variable. But as long as it is exogenous, it does not have any impact on the consistency of the regression coefficients.

② One complication related to the electricity price is the tiered rate structure in the California IOU market, and the fact that those who pay a higher-than-average electricity rate due their larger consumption(and hence a higher rate tier) are also more likely to have installed PV. However, even with detailed time series data for each IOU, the average retail rate that PV adopters are really paying is not obvious without knowing the exact proportion of these customers among different tiers. On the other hand, by assuming that the average rates for PV adopters follow the same trend as the average California residential rates, the regression analysis can capture the true marginal effect.

quarterly data, in both nominal and real terms. The seasonality of the electricity price data is different from the PV installation price; this is why annual data were chosen. Regarding the choice between the nominal price and the real price of electricity, this chapter chose the nominal price series in order to retain the increasing trend in it, which is usually the trend that installers use in their marketing practice. In the main optimization runs, I assume the nominal electricity price to grow by 3% per year(i.e. ρ=0.03). But I also vary it from 0% to 5% in the sensitivity analysis. The rational for checking with a 0% value is because the real electricity price barely increased during the study period and may even have followed a random walk distribution(Anderson et al., 2013).

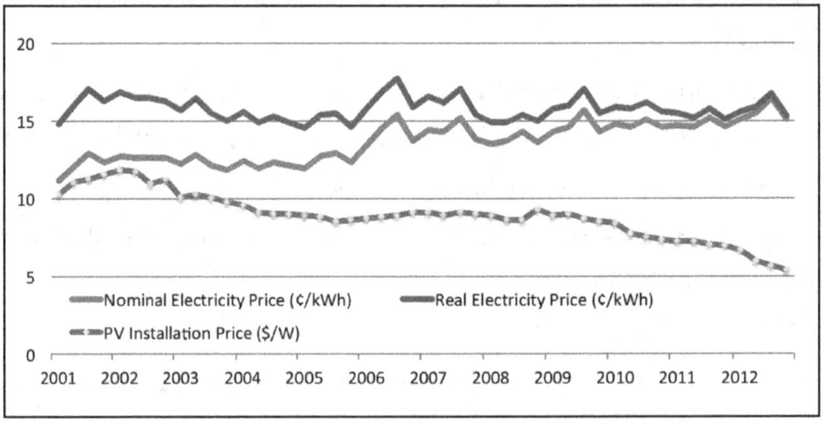

Figure 6 Quarterly California Average Residential Electricity Price Data and PV Installation Price

The ITC variable is derived directly from the stated policy. For California, the state ITC was 15% from 2001 to 2003, and 7.5% for 2004 and 2005. Then, the federal ITC kicked in 2005 with a rate of 30% but imposed a cap of $2,000 from 2005 to 2008. For simplicity, the $2,000 cap is assumed to be always hit, which should be the case since the mean price is higher than $6.67/W before 2009 in California. For 2009 and after, the average ITC is calculated in $/W using information on the net price and the average system size.

Now the DP problem can be solved based on the model setup and parameters obtained. As mentioned above, in order to keep the model aligned with the real CSI decision making, the DP model itself will not include either the ITC or the active number of installers(this is discussed further in Section 3.4.2.1). Also, the coefficients for the variables included will be four times larger than those obtained in Table 3, by converting the quarterly coefficients to annual ones.

4)Results

This section discusses analytic results first, then presents results from the deterministic DP model, and finally introduces uncertainties via stochastic LBD and solves the model again.

(1)Analytic Results

While treating time as continuous and following Kalish and Lilien(1983), the DP model can be rewritten as follows:

$$\max_{\{r(t)\}} x(T)$$

$$\text{s.t.}\dot{x} = f(x,p-r),\ x(0) = x_0$$

$$\dot{y} = rf(x,p-r),\ y(0) = 0,\ y(T) = B$$

where $\dot{x}=\frac{dx}{dt}$ refers to the demand level at time t, f is the demand equation(set to be the constraint(3) in the DP model above), and $\dot{y}$ has the same notation but refers to the budget expenditure.

The Hamiltonian is: $H = \lambda\dot{x} + \phi r\dot{x}$, whereas the co-state variables λ and ϕ are given by: $-\dot{\lambda} = \lambda f_x + \phi r f_x, \lambda(T) = 0$, and ϕ is a negative constant.

Assuming an interior solution exists, the first order condition is:

$H_r = \lambda\frac{\eta f}{r} + \phi f + \phi\eta f = 0$, where $\eta = \frac{\partial f}{\partial p}\frac{p}{f}$ is the usual price elasticity.

It then implies:

$$r = \frac{-\lambda\eta}{\phi(\eta+1)} \tag{7}$$

or $\lambda = \frac{-\phi(\eta+1)r}{\eta}$. I further take second order condition of the Hamiltonian with respect to r:

$$H_{rr} = \lambda\frac{(\eta_r f + \eta f_r)r - \eta f}{r^2} + \phi f_r + \phi(\eta_r f + \eta f_r)$$

into which I plug in λ, and get:

$$H_{rr} = \frac{-\phi(\eta + 1)r}{\eta}\frac{(\eta_r f + \eta f_r)r - \eta f}{r^2} + \phi f_r + \phi(\eta_r f + \eta f_r)$$

$$= \frac{\phi f(\eta + 1)}{r}\left[1 - \frac{\eta_r r}{\eta(\eta + 1)}\right]$$

Since $H_{rr} \leqslant 0$, it implies $K = 1 - \frac{\eta_r r}{\eta(\eta+1)} \geqslant 0$.

The logarithm form of Eq. 7 is:

$$\log(r) = log\left(\frac{-\lambda}{\phi}\right) + \log(\eta) - \log(\eta + 1) \quad (8)$$

Take the total derivative of Eq. 8 with respect to time t:

$$\frac{\dot{r}}{r} = \frac{d(log(r))}{dt} = \frac{\phi}{-\lambda}\frac{-\dot{\lambda}}{\phi} + \frac{\dot{\eta}}{\eta(\eta + 1)}$$

where $\eta = g(x, p-r)$, so that $\dot{\eta} = \frac{d\eta}{dt} = \eta_1 f + \eta_2\dot{p} - \eta_2\dot{r}$. Plug $\dot{\eta}$ and $\dot{\lambda}$ from above into the equation:

$$\frac{\dot{r}}{r} = \frac{\lambda f_x + \phi r f_x}{-\lambda} + \frac{\eta_1 f + \eta_2\dot{p} - \eta_2\dot{r}}{\eta(\eta + 1)}$$

$$= - f_x + \frac{\eta}{\eta + 1}f_x + \frac{\eta_1 f + \eta_2\dot{p}}{\eta(\eta + 1)} - \frac{\eta_2\dot{r}}{\eta(\eta + 1)}$$

Therefore,

$$K\frac{\dot{r}}{r} = \left(1 + \frac{\eta_2 r}{\eta(\eta + 1)}\right)\frac{\dot{r}}{r} = \frac{-f_x}{\eta + 1} + \frac{\eta_1 f}{\eta(\eta + 1)} + \frac{\eta_2 p_x f}{\eta(\eta + 1)}$$

since $\eta_2 = -\eta_r$ and $\dot{p} = \frac{dp}{dx}\frac{dx}{dt} = p_x f$.

Now by definition(Eq. 3), $f = C + \beta_1 x + \beta_2(p-r)$ and $\eta = -\beta_2\frac{p}{f}$, so that:

$$\eta_1 = \frac{d\eta}{dx} = -\beta_2\frac{p_x f - p f_x}{f^2}, \text{ and } \eta_2 = \frac{d\eta}{dp} = -\beta_2\frac{f - \beta_2 p}{f^2} > 0.$$

Thus,

$$K\frac{\dot{r}}{r} = \left(-\frac{1}{\eta+1} + \frac{\beta_2 p}{f^2}\right)f_x + \left(-\frac{\beta_2}{f} + \frac{\eta_2 f}{\eta(\eta+1)}\right)p_x$$
$$\propto \underbrace{\left(-\frac{1}{\eta} + \beta_2\right)}_{<0}\beta_1 + \underbrace{\left(-\beta_2 + \frac{\eta_2}{\eta^2}\right)}_{>0}b \tag{9}$$

since $\beta_2<0$, and $\eta_2>0$. Parameter $b(<0)$ is the learning coefficient as defined in Eq. 4.

The result in Eq. 9 states that, as long as the penetration effect(β_1) is positive, the optimal subsidy/rebate should decrease over time. Furthermore, the bigger the penetration effect, the faster the rebate should decrease. Similar results can be drawn from the learning coefficient term(b); it implies that, if there is a LBD effect, the optimal subsidy/rebate should also be decreasing over time. The greater the(absolute) learning coefficient, the faster it should decrease. Such insights will be revealed again in the following sections when the DP model is solved computationally. Linking back to the parameterization of the LBD coefficient(Section 3.3), using a bigger(in absolute values) than the calculated learning coefficient in this chapter(say 0.15 rather than 0.075) will make the rebate schedule decrease faster.

(2)Deterministic Case

Both basic reasoning and the analytic results suggest that the optimal rebate should decrease over time. The real question is: at what speed? This section utilizes the DP model developed in Section 3.3.1 to answer this question. The DP model is solved with GAMS using the CONOPT solver for nonlinear problems.[①] In this section, I first present the baseline results, and then conduct sensitivity analysis while varying certain key parameters. I further look at the impact of different demand functional forms on the optimal results. Finally, I consider implications of policy flexibility and policy certainty on the optimal subsidy schedule.

①Baseline Results

The baseline results are summarized in Figure 7. While the red bars and

① I also used Excel Solver and R when necessary in solving the model.

lines are for the true CSI, the green versions are the baseline results from the DP optimization. Note that the CSI steps are "collapsed" into annual numbers by taking the averages of the system-level CSI rebate level variable within the same year, which extend for 6 years from 2007 to 2012.① This measurement implicitly accounts for the number of systems of each year and also the proportion of systems at each CSI step within that year.

Compare first the bars for the rebate schedule. The first observation is that the optimal rebate schedule for the DP model provides a much higher rebate at the very beginning and lasts for only 3 years. Although the first number from the optimal rebate may appear to be high($4.2/W versus $2.4/W), it is still realistic considering the PV installation price at that time is as much as $9/W. Even using the net price cutoff point(around $4.7/W) from Drury et al.(2011), this level of subsidy can only make the PV investment cash flow break even.

Similar conclusions have been drawn in the literature for the German FIT(Creti and Joaug, 2012; Lobel and Perakis, 2011). The literature suggests that the optimal FIT in the beginning should be much higher than that used in practice. Creti and Joaug(2012) indicate that the optimal FIT in Germany should have been €1.34/kWh in 2001, much higher than the actual €0.51/kWh. On the other hand, using the logistic function to model the PV demand without necessarily including a penetration effect term usually generates a smoother rebate schedule, as in van Benthem et al.(2008) and Wand and Leuthold(2011) such as environmental externalities and learning-by-doing(LBD) Owing to these potential differences arising from modeling choices, as discussed in Section 3.3 I have considered these issues about parameterization process and robustness checks in depth.

A more appropriate comparison is between how much capacity is installed respectively for these two rebate level schedules, since that is the objective in the first place. In the DP model, changes from the ITC are assumed away, i.e., unless

① CSI was active in 2013 as well. However, this chapter did not make use of 2013 data since it was not available when the research was conducted; in addition, the 2013 average rebate levels were quite low(close to zero).

otherwise stated the reported models assume a constant 30% ITC capped at \$2000 maximum. This is because at the time of CSI design, that was the available information and there was no way to know that the cap will be lifted beginning 2009. Therefore, in the DP model, the ITC term is dropped since—assuming that the \$2000 cap is always hit—it is constant over the time horizon analyzed and will not impact the demand any way. With this assumption, the optimal rebate would incentivize 8.1% more adoption than CSI from 2007 to 2012, which is around 32.2MW, similar to what CSI installed in 2008(32.6MW). Adding the ITC back will generate 28.7MW higher installed capacity from 2009 to 2012, thus, bring the total difference of the optimal schedule to 15.3%(32.2MW + 28.7MW) more compared to CSI.

Since the rebate level is much higher(\$4.2/W) in the first year, the ability of the supply-side(installers) to support the higher level of installations might be a concern. In reality, CSI added around 15MW of under 10kW systems in 2007, but the resultant demand from the optimal solution is 51MW in 2007. This may sound much higher than the CSI number, but ERP and CSI together added around 38MW in 2007. The resulting 51MW is 34.2% higher than this number. In other words, part of the reason why CSI only installed 15MW in 2007 is because ERP was not finished yet. Furthermore, looking at the supply side, a rough count of the active installers in California reveals that the numbers of installers are similar for 2008 and 2004(around 170), even though the actual CSI 2008 installation capacity(32.6MW) is much higher than 2004 ERP number(17.1MW). Thus, it appears that the market should have been able to absorb 51MW in 2007.

As for the \$4.2/W for the first year, the fact that it is even higher than the previous ERP rebate level may sound unacceptable to some extent. Actually, the DP model can easily be constrained to reflect that by requiring the rebate level to be no greater than \$2.5/W. Then, the total adoption is not being maximized anymore; instead, the pace of market development is being controlled. It is obvious that demand is responding to rebate level changes and PV price changes actively, but more importantly demand is also responding to the penetration effects produced by previous demand. That is the key leverage the policymakers are missing during the goal-setting process. Oversubscription did occur at $2.8/W for ERP, but that it was mainly responding to the uncertain policy changes when customers did not know what would happen to them in CSI. In addition, the oversubscription was only temporarily moving the future demand up front, rather than creating new demand. That is another difference between the greater demand from a higher rebate level and the temporary high demand created by impending policy changes.

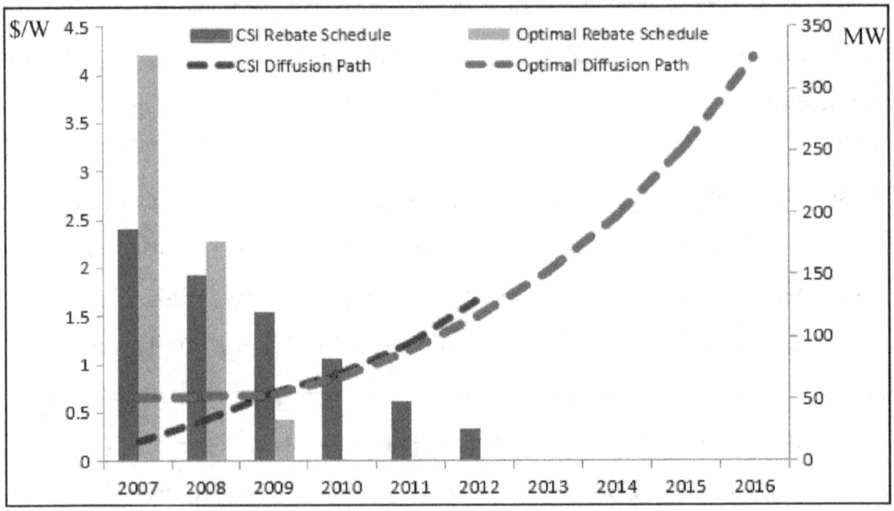

Figure 7 Comparison of the Optimized Baseline Results with the True Annual CSI Schedule

Note in the baseline case: learning coefficient b=−0.075, penetration effect β_1=0.268, and net-price coefficient β_2=−9120. The right axis is the annual level of installations.

②Sensitivity Analysis

The baseline results do not depend much on different parameter values, as can be seen from the sensitivity analysis results in Table 5. I first show the baseline results in terms of the starting rebate level in 2007, number of years offering rebates, the average rebate level through these years, the variance of the rebate series, and lastly the predicted increase of capacity compared to CSI. Then, I vary the learning coefficient(b) from −0.05 to −0.15 in the LBD equation,[①] and the penetration effect coefficient(β_1) from 0.168 to 0.368 in the demand equation. I then vary the growth rate of the electricity price(ρ) from 0% to 5%, and lastly the government discount coefficient(δ) from 0.95 to 1.05[②]. I solve the DP model for the range of values for each parameter, while keeping other parameters at their baseline values.

The overall results are relatively robust to variations in all of the key parameters I examined. The starting rebate levels are almost all above $4/W, and seldom do the rebates last longer than three years. The average rebate levels are higher than CSI because of the shorter duration, whereas the variances in the rebate schedules are greater than CSI. Lastly, the capacity achievements differ from case to case, but generally outperform CSI except for two extreme cases.[③]

The penetration effect seems to be most influential in determining the optimal rebate schedule and the installed capacity trajectory. Consistent with the analytical results presented earlier, when the penetration effect is stronger, the rebate rate decreases more quickly, and PV adoption grows more quickly. On the other hand, a smaller penetration effect can make the rebate schedule longer lasting and smoother. Similarly, a stronger LBD brings about the same phenomenon, but not as dramatically as with the stronger penetration effect. In addition, the electricity rate increase seems not to impact the optimal rebate schedule significantly, but mainly shifts the demand in a relatively exogenous manner. Finally, different government discount coefficients produce results very similar to the baseline model.

---

① The learning coefficient range [0.05,0.15] is consistent with realistic learning coefficients for a range of technologies considered in the literature, including PV(Jamasb and Kohler, 2008; Kohler et al., 2006).

② I consider a greater than 1 value for δ to account for the likely potential scenario in which technological change increases the efficiency of solar panels so that the same capacity yields different amounts of power generation.

③ Recall that these capacity estimates are without including the federal ITC, which is known to have had a significant effect on installations(see Section 3.4.2.1). As such, the findings reported in Table 5 are conservative estimates. For example, in the presence of the ITC, one of the extreme cases(ρ=0) is comparable to the actual CSI outcome.

The overall finding is that the optimal rebate levels seem to be higher at the beginning and then decrease more quickly than the actual CSI levels in order to spur maximum PV diffusion; this is due to the presence of(strong) penetration effects and LBD. One technical explanation for the steeper rebate curve is that the marginal effect of increasing the subsidy level is almost zero starting from period four, thus making the subsidy less useful or even meaningless. Also, the positive marginal effect in periods two and three suggest that the risk of a corner solution is negligible. This is because of the nonlinear LBD constraint in the DP model and also the fact that it is relatively cheaper to subsidize later PV adoption.

Table 5 Sensitivity Analysis Results with Different Parameters

	Starting rebate ($/W)	Years of rebate	Average rebate ($/W)	Rebate variance	Capacity increase (relative to CSI)
CSI	2.40	6	1.31	0.52	0
Baseline	4.20	3	2.30	2.38	8.13%
$b=-0.05$	4.14	3	2.36	2.08	2.86%
$b=-0.05$	4.38	2	3.22	1.35	23.8%
$\beta_1=0.168$	3.80	4	2.19	1.40	−31.6%
$\beta_1=0.368$	4.38	2	2.94	2.08	66.2%
$\rho=0$	4.12	3	2.46	1.81	−8.47%
$\rho=0.05$	4.28	3	2.21	2.83	20.2%
$\delta=0.95$	4.23	3	2.30	2.47	8.13%
$\delta=1.05$	4.18	3	2.31	2.33	8.13%

In the event that a(strong) penetration effect exists, subsidizing more at an earlier stage could generate multiple benefits: one direct and two indirect. The direct effect is that, by offsetting the high price, a subsidy can spur demand by itself. The two indirect effects are through(i) the penetration effect, whereby subsequent adopters face lower costs because more customers have adopted solar before them, and(ii) the higher induced price reduction, where more early adoption lowers the price faster via LBD. All three benefits drive more subsidies to be spent at the beginning. Within the demand model used here(Eq. 3), the same rebate level can only incentivize demand by the same amount irrespective of whether the rebate is being assigned to the present or to the future(ignoring all those indirect effects), because the coefficient is constant and the same for both cases. However, one of the disadvantages of subsidizing in the future is that the demand level will likely be much higher than the beginning periods, thus requiring more funding in absolute numbers. Other than changing how the rebate variable enters the demand equation, from an optimality perspective there are hardly any reasons why the decision maker should spread the subsidy more evenly. Of course, in the reality of complex decision-making processes and program design, where considerations of simplicity, flexibility, and certainty are very important, spreading the subsidy more evenly might appear to the decision-makers as a better option.

As to the two concerns regarding(i) the option value and(ii) the rebate-price interaction(or the rebate/price ratio) term implying that a small level but a large proportion of rebate(relative to the installation price) will generate more adoption, this chapter found neither of these is a substantial effect(Table 4). While the DP model presented here is probably not the best model to estimate the option value(see Burr, 2012), I do not find any postponed buying effect. On the contrary, some literature actually finds the so-called “Announcement Effect”(Gürtler and Sieg, 2010), which refers to the rushing up(of application and adoption) right before the announcement of reducing the rebate is made. This also happens to CSI, as found in Hughes and Podolefsky(2013). In other words, consumers did not wait to buy in order to explore the option value, but did the opposite. As to the rebate-price interaction, the robustness check in the demand equation suggests that such an interaction(or ratio) term is statistically insignificant and thus can be ignored(see Table 4 and its discussion for more details).

③Other Demand Functional Forms

To further test the robustness of the findings, I bring in other demand functional forms that I initially considered in Table 3. I show the respective optimal rebate schedule for each of them along with the baseline model in Figure 8. All models show higher-than-CSI starting rebate level and shorter-than-CSI policy duration. The similarity between the baseline model and the R-L model is much higher than others. Furthermore, using the compound NPV measure instead of the individual value components puts more emphasis on early-time subsidization, as shown by the starting rebate level for nearly \$6/W and the two-year policy effective time. This is due to the negative NPV in 2007, which has the effect of reducing PV adoption with a positive coefficient in the demand equation; thus, in this case, it makes more sense to subsidize heavily at the very beginning to make the NPV positive.

When comparing the linear functional form for the Baseline and NPV models versus their log-linear forms, the results indicate a smoother rebate schedule for the latter, i.e. the rebate starts lower and lasts longer. These results are understandable because the log-linear functional form implicitly assumes that the same rebate level will incentivize more PV adoption in future time periods than current: i.e., when the installation base is bigger, the same percentage of newly spurred adoption(by any demand factor) means more PV installations. The starting rebate levels for these two log-linear models are between \$3.5/W and \$3.6/W, which is much higher than \$2.4/W within CSI. Overall, different functional forms for PV demand do not change the major conclusions.

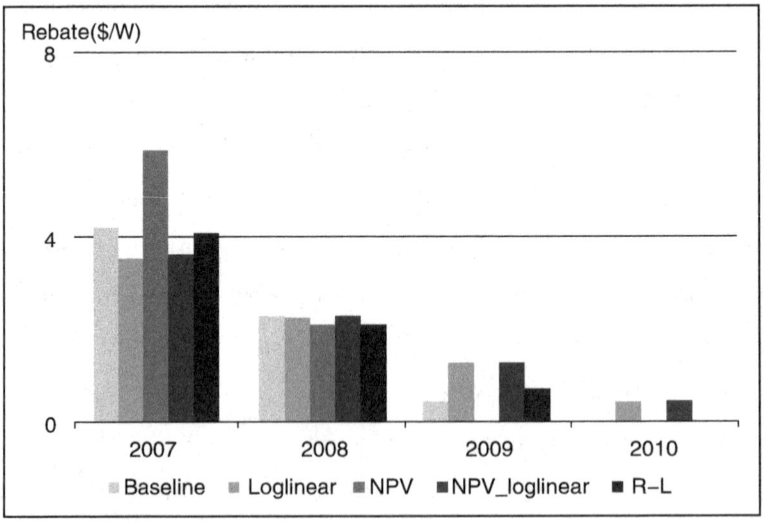

Figure 8 Optimal Rebate Schedule for Different PV Demand Models

④Policy Flexibility Consideration

In investigating 'policy flexibility' I try to address the following question: how would the optimal rebate schedule change if rebates could be adjusted more frequently, i.e. on a quarterly rather than a yearly basis? Since the PV market has been evolving rapidly, adapting the rebate level according to existing market conditions could potentially bring additional benefits in terms of spurring adoption. The linear functional form in the baseline model① and availability of quarterly data allow us to address this question. Accordingly, to model the policy flexibility scenario I use the original regression coefficients for the demand equation(Eq. 3) without multiplying them by four to obtain the yearly coefficients.

The optimal rebate schedule with policy flexibility consideration is depicted in Figure 9 on a quarterly basis, along with the CSI rebates. One interesting finding is that the rebate still lasts for roughly three years, same as the baseline model. Furthermore, the starting rebate level is relatively higher(≈\$5/W) compared to the baseline model(≈\$4/W). Regarding the scale of installations, the performance of the policy flexibility case is much better than the baseline model; compared to the CSI case, it further incentivizes 26.4% more adoption(around 105MW more). This should not come as any surprise because policy flexibility as modeled here essentially means greater ability to set rebate levels closer to market conditions, thereby enabling higher PV diffusion. On the flip side, the real quarterly PV demand curve shows much larger variation than the yearly version(Figure 7), indicating potentially more administrative work in adjusting rebate levels in practice.

Note that in the policy flexibility case, learning coefficient b=−0.075, other demand-related parameters are set four times smaller than the baseline case: penetration effect β_1=0.067, and net-price coefficient β_2=−2280. The right axis is the quarterly level of installations.

⑤Policy Certainty Consideration

Policy certainty is also considered an important feature of subsidy

① The linear demand functional form is advantageous in this case since the estimated coefficients can be converted back and forth between using quarterly data and using annual data.

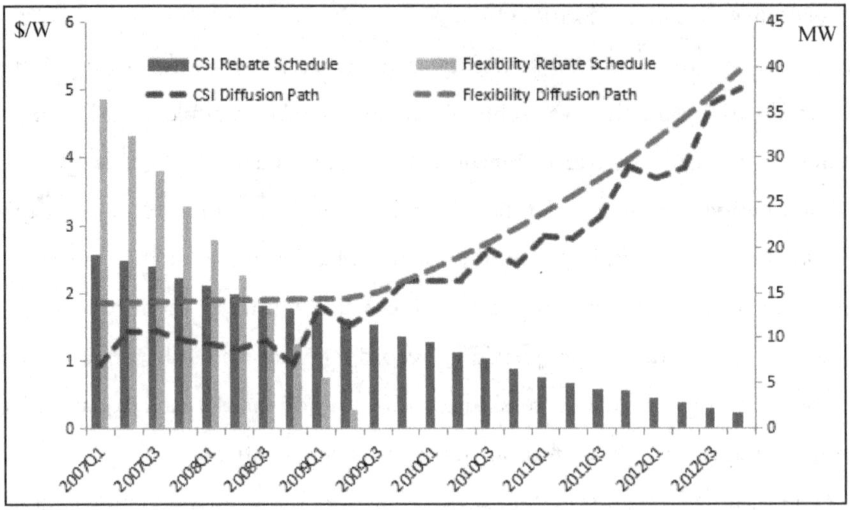

Figure 9 Optimal Rebate with Policy Flexibility Consideration

policies(Klein et al., 2008; Sawin, 2004), although different decision-makers might have different weighting matrices how much they value policy certainty. Following the DP model setup, policy certainty requires that the rebate level not drop too much from one step to the next, which can be modeled by adding the variance of the rebate variable to the objective function.① Since the optimal rebate generally decreases over time, the variance term should control for the pace of dropping sufficiently. Of course, some weight needs to be attached to such a variance term, to ensure that the rebate variance term and the cumulative installed PV capacity have the same magnitude(or scale). This process can be calibrated to extract how much weight CSI may be putting on the consideration of policy certainty.②

Still using the baseline setup, Figure 10 shows a roughly similar trajectory of rebates to CSI. The PV adoption is similar to CSI as well, only 1.7% lower. To be clear,

---

① In explicit forms, the new objective function would be: $\max_{\{r_t\}}\left(\sum_{t=1}^{T}\delta^t q(r)_t+\lambda\cdot var(r_t)\right)$, where a calibrated weight term is attached to the new variance term of the rebate time series.

② Some experimentation is required with the weight for the variance termof the rebate series to make sure that the total capacity and the variance of the rebate series have roughly the same magnitude. In my case the results were obtained using a weight of 1 : 180, since the capacity is in MW.

the policy certainty rebate level is often lower than the CSI case, because PV adoption is higher at the beginning and costs more as a result. Comparing the policy certainty scenario with the baseline DP scenario, PV adoption drops by almost 10%(1.7%+8.1%), which then may be viewed as "the cost of policy certainty"(or any other concerns).

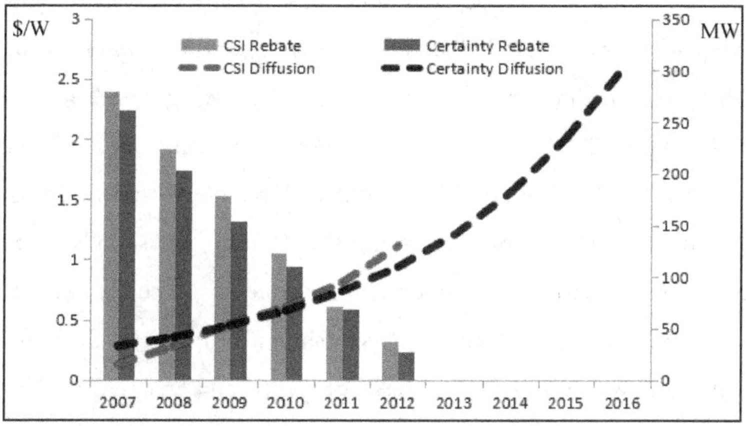

Figure 10 Optimal Rebate with Policy Certainty Consideration

Note that in the policy certainty case, parameters are set the same as the baseline case: learning coefficient b=−0.075, penetration effect β_1=0.268, and net-price coefficient β_2=−9120, except that the former adopts a slightly different objective that values both the cumulative installed capacity and the policy certainty. The right axis is the annual level of installations.

(3)Stochastic Case

As evident in Figure 5, the price dynamics cannot be fully captured only by the cumulative capacity(in lag term). Two approaches to model the dynamics more accurately include: (i) an additive noise term(ω_t) or, (ii) by allowing the learning coefficient to time-varying(b_t).① The model is then learning these parameters

① Note the difference here with the broad literature on either stochastic programming or stochastic dynamic programming: I only characterize the uncertainty with its central tendency term(i.e. the mean), rather than a discrete probabilistic distribution. Results on the later approach are available upon request, and the optimal rebate schedule looks similar to that presented in this subsection.

through time, although with some lags.[①] The following assumes a 1-year lag for such learning. The first case is to introduce an additive noise term from last period to the current LBD prediction based on Eq. 4. The additive noise term is: $\omega_{t-1} = p_{t-1} - p^*_{t-1}$, where p_{t-1} and p^*_{t-1}, are the observed and predicted price from last period. So, for example, at the beginning of 2007 the policymakers can observe p_{2006} and estimate the LBD equation using data till 2006 to predict p^*_{2006}, and thus calculate ω_{2006} . They will use this term to adjust the prediction of p^*_{2007} by adding them together to form a new prediction for 2007: $p^{*'}_{2007}=p^*_{2007}+\omega_{2006}$. With new data from 2007, this process can move on by itself. One rational for this additive noise adjustment is that it is highly possible that the learning-by-doing shock terms are serially correlated, so that one can use the last-period shock term to predict the current shock term. In other words, the shock is not random, as is shown in Figure 5. Similar stochastic LBD via the additive noise term has been proposed and analyzed by Mazzola and McCardle(1996; 1997), although not in any computational framework.

The multiplicative uncertain case through b_t is a little more complicated. First, a dynamic regression model(DRM) version of the LBD equation must be estimated, through which the time-varying coefficient b_t is obtained. The DRM model can be specified as follows:

$$d\_log(p_t) = b_t log(Q_{t-1}) + \theta_t \tag{10}$$

$$b_t = b_{t-1} + \zeta_t \tag{11}$$

where $\theta_t \sim N(0, \phi_t)$ and $\zeta_t \sim N(0, \psi_t)$. The dependent variable $d\_log(p_t)$ is the demeaned version of the series $log(p_t)$, i.e. $d\_log(p_t) = log(p_t) - mean(log(p_t))$. Such transformation is neat in getting rid of the intercept term. The end results of the DRM model is the time-varying coefficients b_t, which follows an AR(1)process as specified in Eq. 11.

① One can use the same technique to model possible uncertainties in the demand equation; however, it has to consider the possible connection between ERP and CSI and its implications on modeling the uncertain demand for CSI. Also, the demand equation has more than one independent variable, which will create more complexities if introducing multiplicative uncertainties. In any case, the demand side appears to be less uncertain, since the demand curve is smoother and, thus, is easier to predict.

Similar to the additive noise case, I impose a 1-year lag for the learning of this time-varying LBD coefficient. For example, at the beginning of 2007, the coefficient b_{2006} is known and imported to LBD equation(Eq. 4) for 2007; together with information on the cumulative installed capacity in 2006, i.e. Q_{2006}, I obtain the predicted price b_{2007}. For the following years, I only know the LBD coefficients, without knowing the installed capacity in those years. Therefore, I ask the DP model to take the LBD coefficients as given(still with a 1-year lag),① and then solve for the optimal rebate and PV installed capacity starting from 2007.

The above DRM approach is useful in specifying a time-varying LBD coefficient series; however, it is suboptimal in the sense that the coefficient estimation is not updated with new information from the DP model, i.e. those newly obtained annual installed capacity from 2007 to 2012. Since there is only one independent variable in the LBD regression, a better way to incorporate this new information is backward induction(BI)②, which basically derives the learning coefficient via dividing the dependent variable(de-meaned log price) by the independent variable(log past cumulative capacity) for each time period to obtain the seemingly "perfect" coefficient. As a result of this derivation, the dependent variable is completely explained and the random noise term becomes essentially zero. In addition, such BI derivationcan be simply looped together with the optimization process.

The BI plus DP algorithm can be summarized as follows:

---

① Lucas Critique may apply to this(Lucas Jr, 1976), which basically says that new policies could change important behavior patterns and thus coefficients in the specified econometric models; thus rendering the optimization results from the model with constant coefficients useless. However, I think time-varying coefficients are less vulnerable to such critique than a constant coefficient. In addition, as discussed next, I also use a different method that loops the parameter estimation and optimization together. One can potentially test the bias from DRM, which is found to be small since the learning coefficients are relatively stable during the period of decision-making.

② Note that Backward Induction here is different from the similar concept in the framework of dynamic programming, where backward induction is one of the main methods for solving the Bellman equation using the ending condition.

- Run the regression(Eq. 10) using data till 2006, and obtain LBD coefficient ;
- Use b_{2006} and Q_{2006} to predict p^{*}_{2007}, and inject it to the DP model;
- Set an initial value for the rebate as r^{0}_{2007} and then calculate q^{0}_{2007} and Q^{0}_{2007} based on Eq. 3 and Eq. 2 respectively;
- Run the regression(Eq. 10) using data till 2006 plus p^{*}_{2007} and Q_{2006}, and obtain b_{2007};
- Loop over(2)~(4) for 2008 and forwards;
- Search for r_t that maximizes for $\delta^{T}Q_{T}$ from t 2007 to 2012.

As such, the DP model is solved, which is again looped together with the LBD coefficient estimation process. New information on annual installed capacity starting from 2007 is used in each year's BI derivation. Actually, I have used all the information on the price and the capacity series prior to 2007 to predict the installation price in 2007. This process goes on for future years with new capacity information obtained from the DP model. Note that this is not necessarily the actual capacity numbers in the real world, because the rebate schedule has been changed.

Figure 11 compares the learning coefficients from these three approaches: simple OLS(this is the baseline case), DRM, and BI. Note that the BI coefficients in Figure 11 do not utilize any results from the optimization process for either the price term or the cumulative capacity term. I use the observed data on these two terms to calculate the BI coefficients, merely to show the stochasticity in the coefficient itself. It turns out that the learning coefficients for both DRM and BI were relative smaller in absolute values from 2006 to 2009, meaning the learning effects were weaker. After that, the learning effect picked up again. In the stochastic optimization framework, results from either the dynamic regression or BI are used and then compared to the additive noise case.

The stochastic optimization results are summarized in Figure 12. Although the learning coefficient exhibits certain variation in Figure 11, it is still relatively weak compared to the strong penetration effects, in the sense that the results in the uncertainty scenarios are similar to the baseline case. The first rebate levels for the four cases are: \$4.20 for the baseline case, \$4.108 for the additive noise case, \$4.198

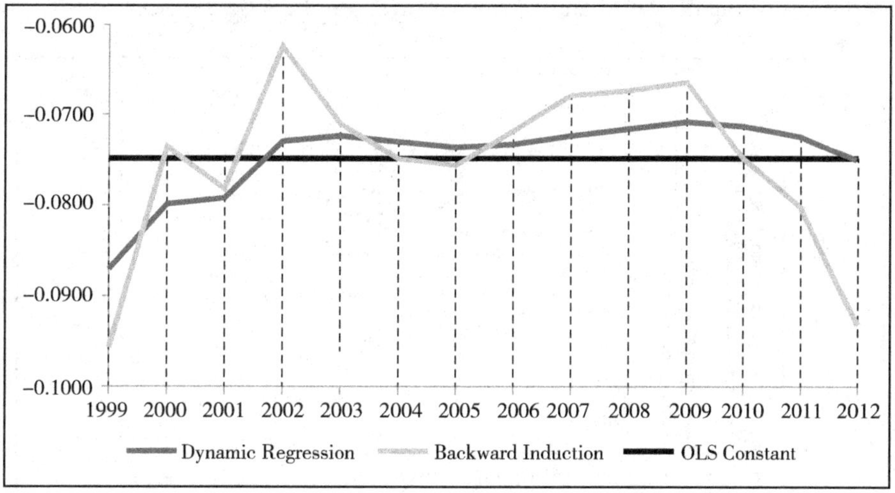

Figure 11 Dynamic LBD Parameters without Updating from Optimization

for DRM, and $4.169 for BI. The relatively low value for the additive noise case is because the observed installation price in 2006 was higher than predicted from the model, resulting in a lower marginal effect of increasing the rebate level in 2007. Then, since the spurred demand(as a result of a lower rebate level) was smaller, so were the potential penetration benefits. All the other three cases(Baseline, DRM and BI)do not exhibit a similar trend. The DRM and BI case, however, may somewhat reflect this trend because of a relatively lower learning coefficient compared to later years(in absolute values). On the other hand, the similarities between DRM, BI, and the baseline case are because of rather stable learning phenomenon from 2006 to 2009, and because they are relatively close to the assumed constant one in the baseline case(Figure 11). While DRM is closer to the baseline case in Figure 11, that is also why the optimal rebate schedules of these two stay close to each other(Figure 12). Comparing DRM and BI cases with the additive noise case, the main observation is that the estimated dynamic learning coefficient is relatively stable in the DRM and BI cases compared to the random shock term in the additive noise case; similarly, the optimal rebate schedule results in the DRM and BI case are closer to the baseline results than the additive noise case. Furthermore, when stochasticity of this learning coefficient is larger, it may become more rational to wait and see, thus distinguishing the DRM and BI cases more from the baseline case.

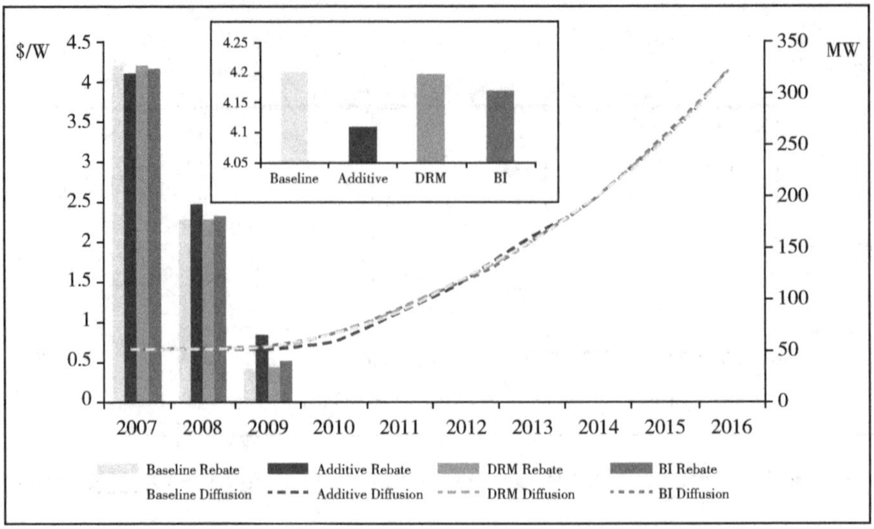

Figure 12 DP Results with Additive Noise or Time-varying LBD Parameters

Note that learning coefficient b=−0.075, penetration effect β_1=0.268, and net-price coefficient β_2=−9120, and the other three cases differ in the LBD equation, either adding an additive noise term or making the learning coefficient dynamic. The right axis is the annual level of installations.

So far, the impact of uncertainties has been demonstrated with respect to the LBD equation. The results indicate that, under uncertainties, the optimal rebate schedule could be a little more "conservative"(more spread out compared to the baseline case), responding to the relative plateau of installation price from 2007 to 2009. Instead, if one did not update the additive noises or the learning coefficient year by year with new data, but rather assumed a certain distribution of the random noise term or the learning coefficient, then the optimal rebate schedule would look even smoother(i.e., more spread out or "conservative"). However, generally researchers consider LBD to be a constant phenomenon and often the learning effect is actually expected to be stronger(e.g. van Benthem et al., 2008; Wand and Leuthold, 2011). In any of these cases, the results of this chapter stand well and may even represent somewhat conservative estimates of the optimal solutions.

5)Conclusions

In this chapter, I address the design of optimal subsidy schedules for encouraging the adoption of renewable energy technologies like solar PV. Following closely the logic and design of the California Solar Initiative, I develop a dynamic programming(DP) framework to maximize the total installed capacity under the CSI budget constraint. I obtain robust parameters for the DP model, and present both analytical and computational results.

There are some limitations to my modeling approach. First, it is plausible that the policy process may have other objectives than just trying to achieve optimal deployment as defined and modeled here. For example, one objective could be policy certainty and the health of the supply chain(installers) over program timeline. While I have explored the former case in my study, a fully resolved model of other objectives would be much more complex, as it would require modeling the market structure explicitly as part of the DP framework. Our study could still serve as a basic framework and can be extended to incorporate additional considerations. Second, although uncertainty on the demand side is relatively small compared with potential supply-side dynamics(such as price shocks), my modeling finds demand-side parameters to be quite important in the determining the final outcome. Thus, it may be useful to include more sources of uncertainties in the model, especially for the demand equation(and the electricity price term) either through a time-varying coefficient or an additive noise term. Finally, when incorporating uncertainties, one needs to be careful about the Lucas critique. I used the method of Backward Induction to get around this issue, but the situation may be different and more challenging in other cases.

Our analytical results indicate that in the presence of penetration effects, the optimal subsidy level should decrease over time. Based on the parameter estimation, the penetration effects are indeed found to be strong and stable after controlling for other factors. The insights from the analytical model are consistent with the computational results: as expected, the optimal CSI rebate schedule I obtain decreases over time, but it does so much more quickly than the implemented CSI policy. Similar conclusions are found in the literature for the German feed-in-tariff(Creti and Joaug, 2012; Lobel and Perakis, 2011). As a result, the cumulative CSI installed capacity from 2007 to 2012 could have increased by 8.1%(comparable to the CSI MW installation in 2008), even without considering the positive change that happened to the federal ITC in 2009. Sensitivity analysis tested the results in response to variations in different parameters, but no substantial changes occurred to the optimal rebate trajectory, not even with a much lower penetration effect. Our results are also robust to different PV demand functional forms. I further explore commonly cited concerns that likely guided the design of CSI: providing policy flexibility and certainty. Including policy flexibility – by letting the rebate level drop in ten steps-into the policy design stimulates significantly more PV adoption compared to the baseline case. On the other hand, after including policy certainty into the objective—by keeping rebates from dropping dramatically between the various steps—the optimal rebate schedule starts to look like the implemented CSI, both of which come at the "cost" of 10% lower installed cumulative capacity relative to the optimal baseline case.

The results from the stochastic case after introducing uncertainties to LBD are not substantially different from the baseline case, with respect to either the additive uncertainty case or the multiplicative uncertainty case. That is because the uncertainty term keeps being updated over time using new information from the data, which ultimately gets close to the deterministic case, in which all the information have been used. Another reason for this similarity is that the LBD dynamics stays rather stable from 2007 to 2009, resulting in a relatively small uncertainty term, whose effect is then dominated by penetration effects. As known from the deterministic case, the latter primarily determines the shape of the rebate schedule, even with a relatively small parameter value.

Based on these results, I offer some suggestions for subsidy policy design related to renewable energy technologies:

• Trying to set up the budget, capacity target, and timeline for a rebate schedule simultaneously will result in one element being out of control. This is obvious, but worth reiterating that not all these factors may be controlled at the same time.

• Tailoring the subsidy level to the potential demand situation increases program efficiency. This is especially relevant in situations where strong penetrations effects may exist. In those cases demand is usually higher than otherwise expected, especially during the later periods when the penetration effects become even stronger. Generally, in these situations more of the budget should be shifted to earlier periods.

• Uncertainties generally discourage people from adopting novel technologies. Obviously, there is no shortcut to control for uncertainties, but I find that from an efficiency perspective it is a good strategy to keep updating some of the key parameters on both supply and demand side assumptions. Using more data obtained from the operational phase of subsidy programs will bring the results closer to the optimal case. However, there may be a tradeoff here with the certainty element of the program.

Chapter 4 Incentive Pass-through for Residential Solar Systems in California

1)Introduction

The deployment of solar photovoltaic(PV) has grown rapidly over the last decade. While global annual installed PV capacity was less than 0.3 gigawatts(GW) in 2000, this number surpassed 38GW in 2013(EPIA, 2014). Deployment in the United States has also grown rapidly, from around 0.004GW of newly installed capacity in 2000 to more than 4GW in 2013(Sherwood, 2013; SEIA/GTM, 2014). A key driving force behind such growth has been the myriad of government incentive programs promoting solar deployment, often motivated by a desire to address two possible market failures indirectly: the unpriced environmental consequences of conventional energy sources(Bezdek, 1993; Painuly, 2002) and learning-by-doing and innovation spillover effects in the PV industry(McDonald and Schrattenholzer, 2001; van Benthem et al., 2008). Other factors driving policy decisions to support solar include the potential benefits of energy resource diversity and the possibility of new jobs and economic activity in the solar sector.[①]

Many federal and state programs in the United States offer financial

① Many economists would question whether direct support for the solar sector is the most efficient mechanism for correcting market failures, and they would also question whether some of the policy motivations listed here even call for government intervention(e.g., jobs and economic activity).

incentives(often in the form of up-front rebates) to remove capital barriers for customers to adopt PV. With a budget of more than $2 billion and a program life of a decade(2007—2016), the California Solar Initiative(CSI) is a good example of a large-scale U.S. program. The major aim of the CSI is to spur solar deployment, with a goal of 1.94GW of new solar capacity by 2016(CPUC, 2014). However, the degree to which the financial incentives offered by the CSI have been actually passed through to PV customers is an open question. In practice, though PV customers could apply for the incentives directly, the vast majority instead authorizes PV installers to submit incentive claims on their behalf; the PV installers then provide PV customers a discount on the installation prices that is equal to the incentive received. Even in this case, it is unclear whether incentives are fully passed through to customers, because installers may opt to adjust their pre-incentive PV prices to account for those incentives. The pass-through rate, therefore, crucially depends on how PV installers determine pre-incentive PV prices. If PV installers price their systems on a pre-incentive basis higher when incentives are larger, then PV customers will not benefit fully from the provision of the incentives, and instead installers will retain some fraction of the available incentive. This especially might be the case if PV installers face high customer demand for PV and low demand elasticity.

This report focuses on the incentive pass-through question for the CSI while also using data from the previous residential incentive program in California—the Emerging Renewables Program(ERP)—because these two programs are collectively the largest and longest-running state-level PV incentive programs in the United States. Previous studies that have used California's solar installation data to conduct various types of econometric analyses include Bollinger and Gillingham(2012), Burr(2012), Henwood(2014), Hughes and Podolefsky(2013), and van Benthem et al.(2008). Our work leverages the sizable dataset of system-level PV prices managed by Lawrence Berkeley National Laboratory(LBNL), and is part of a larger body of research conducted by LBNL, Yale University, University of Wisconsin, and University of Texas at Austin that is exploring, more broadly, the drivers of PV price variability in the United States. Our focus here is on residential PV systems in California, and I exclude "appraised value" third-party-owned(TPO) PV systems; as such, the pass-through rates estimated here do not apply outside of California or to appraised-value TPO systems. Moreover, the results presented here focus narrowly on the pass-through rate for direct solar incentives offered by the CSI and ERP. I do not evaluate value-based pricing more broadly, considering the combined impact of direct state incentives, electric utility bill savings, and federal tax incentives.

The nine step changes in CSI(also called "step-downs", see Figure 1 for more details)provide sufficient variation of rebates over time and between utilities to study the question of incentive pass-through(also called "subsidy pass-through" or "subsidy incidence"), i.e., how much of the incentive has been passed through to PV consumers. This concept of incentive pass-through is analogous to that of tax pass-through(also called "tax incidence"), where the question is whether consumers or suppliers bear a tax burden, and has been used in a wide variety of other contexts. Early work on tax incidence includes Due(1954), Brownlee and Perry(1967), and Woodard and Siegelman(1967); Section 4.2 discusses additional literature in this area. Pass-through rates have been commonly evaluated either through structural modeling or reduced-form regression analysis, and I use both methods in the present study. Regression discontinuity(RD) designs have also often been employed to evaluate pass-through rates; though I do not implement such designs in the present analysis, chapter 5 uses RD analysis and obtains pass-through estimates that are similar to those presented in this chapter.

Though the CSI has now wound down as final solar capacity targets have been reached, estimating the historical pass-through rate has important broader implications for solar policy design. The question of the relative distribution of incentives to PV customers and PV installers should be an important aspect of the CSI policy evaluation, especially as policymakers would presumably prefer that solar incentives are largely passed through to the intended recipients: PV customers. Moreover, incentive programs of various types still exist in the U.S. and other countries; thus, the historical performance of the CSI is relevant not only as an ex-post analysis in California, but potentially has broader policy implications for other solar incentive programs both nationally and internationally. Understanding the pass-through rate also illuminates the level of competition in local solar markets and, therefore, may help guide solar deployment policy efforts. In particular, if the pass-through rate is found to be low(i.e., a large portion of the incentive is absorbed by installers), this may tell policymakers to focus more of their efforts on lowering entry barriers and increasing competition among PV installers. On the other hand, a high pass-through rate might be an indication of a smoothly functioning incentive program.

The rest of the report is organized as follows. In Section 4.2, I summarize the pass-through literature, including both theoretical and empirical work. Section 4.3 discusses the methods and underlying data. In Section 4.4, I show the main results for the CSI/ERP incentive pass-through rate estimation, and I compare the pass-through rates estimated by structural modeling and reduced-form regression. I conclude the report in Section 4.5.

2)Literature Review

Similar to tax pass-through, the incentive pass-through rate(PT) can be formally defined as:

$$PT = -\frac{d(Net\ Price)}{d(Incentive)} \times 100\% \tag{12}$$

i.e., the(absolute)marginal impact of incentive changes on the net(post-incentive) price paid by consumers. A pass-through rate of 100% implies that incentives are fully passed through to customers, whereas a rate of less than 100% means that some portion of the incentives is retained by the PV installer.

Sometimes, researchers instead study variations in pre-incentive prices(not net, post-incentive prices); in this case, the pass-through rate can still be derived from the results, since:

$$PT = -\frac{d(Price - Incentive)}{d(Incentive)} \times 100\% = \left(1 - \frac{d(Price)}{d(Incentive)}\right) \times 100\% \tag{13}$$

In other words, the pass-through rate in this instance is one minus the coefficient on the incentive term(in the regression of pre-incentive prices), which is then multiplied by 100%.

In public economics theory, researchers have derived the pass-through rate based on the curvature of demand and production cost curves as well as the level of market competition(Delipalla and Keen, 1992; Fullerton and Metcalf, 2002; Sijm et al., 2012; Stern, 1987; Vivid Economics, 2007). Essentially, pass-through is a market-equilibrium concept. In the case of PV incentives, those incentives may act as a positive demand shifter(increasing demand for PV), but they might also impact PV costs depending on the shape of the marginal cost curve. In addition to demand and production cost curvature, the level of market competition also plays a key role in determining the pass-through rate.

Since pass-through is an equilibrium concept, it becomes necessary to estimate demand, supply, and equilibrium conditions simultaneously. Figure 13 provides a simple illustration of the incentive pass-through concept. With a linear supply curve(or marginal cost function) and a linear demand curve in two periods, the pass-through rate is equal to the absolute change in net price paid by consumers(ΔNP) divided by the incentive level change(R). In a more-flexible(and not necessarily linear) supply and demand framework, this is the same as taking the first derivative of net price with respect to the incentive(Eq. 12). This line of argument ties closely to assessing market power using the elasticity-adjusted Lerner index,① also called the "conduct" or "market power" parameter(Genesove and Mullin, 1998; Wolfram, 1999).② Furthermore, estimating pass-through rates has strong implications for

① The Lerner index describes a firm's market power, measured by(price-marginal cost)/price. The index ranges from 0 to 1, i.e., the percentage of the firm's mark-up to the price.

② The conduct parameter approach was previously known as the conjecture variation approach, which was not without debates in the literature. While there are several outstanding critiques of this approach(Corts, 1999; Reiss and Wolak, 2007), other literature tends to justify its evolutionary consistency(Dixon and Somma, 2003; Possajennikov, 2009; Rachapalli and Kulshreshtha, 2013). Based on Jaffe and Weyl(2013), there was a recent resurgence in studies using this approach, both theoretical and empirical(see references cited there).

various welfare analyses and market-design problems(Weyl and Fabinger, 2013).

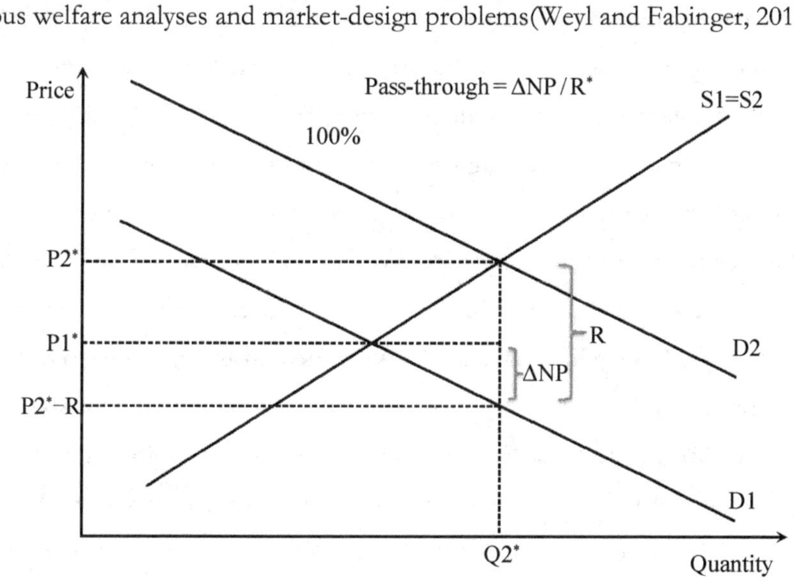

Figure 13 Equilibrium Depiction of Incentive Pass-through

Note: The introduced incentive level R in period 2 moves the demand curve from D1 to D2, and a new market equilibrium emerges at(P2*, Q2*) assuming the supply curve remains the same: S1 = S2. The net price paid by consumers in period 1 is the market price P1*, while in period 2 it is(P2* − R), so the absolute net price change is ΔNP. Though this logic applies to an increase in incentive levels, the order of time can be reversed to create a similar case for incentive-level reductions.

Empirically, there are two ways to estimate the pass-through rate. The first is to estimate the pass-through rate through structural modeling, where researchers impose theoretical assumptions on the demand function, production technology, and how suppliers maximize profits responding to others' change in market behaviors. Genesove and Mullin(1998) applied this method with various functional forms for demand to the refined sugar industry and verified it with reliable marginal cost data. Barnett et al.(1995) used a translog functional form for the production cost and compared cigarette tax incidence between the federal level and the state level. Other similar work includes Besley and Rosen(1999), Bettendorf and Verboven(2000), Clay and Troesken(2003), and Karp and Perloff(1989), among others. Somewhat differently, Bergin and Feenstra(2009) derived the pass-through rate in a monopolistic competition framework. Further, Kim and Cotterill(2008) used a discrete choice demand model(following Berry et al., 1995) for processed cheese and estimated pass-through rates for input-cost changes. To date, no structural-modeling work has been done for solar incentive pass-through.

The second method for estimating pass-through is by employing a reduced-form regression analysis to estimate the marginal impact of a tax(or incentive) on consumer prices. Researchers have applied this method to study the pass-through question for various taxes(Besley and Rosen, 1999; Carbonnier, 2007; Marion and Muehlegger, 2011; Poterba, 1996), exchange rates(Choudhri and Hakura, 2012; Gopinath et al., 2010; Marazzi et al., 2005), and upstream cost shocks(Alexeeva-Talebi, 2011; Gron and Swenson, 2000; Vavra and Goodwin, 2005). Several studies have also looked at incentive pass-through specifically, focusing on, for example, federal tax credits for the Toyota Prius(Sallee, 2011), agricultural subsidies to farmland(Kirwan, 2009; Hendricks et al., 2012), and automobile manufacturer promotions(Busse et al., 2006). Though difference-in-difference and fixed-effects models are typically used in these regression analyses, few make the explicit connection between these work and the pass-through theory in public economics.

As for solar incentives, a few studies have looked at the pass-through question with reduced-form regression analysis. Several unpublished works have studied the question using CSI data(Henwood, 2014; Peterman, 2012; Podolefsky, 2013). Podolefsky(2013) found a low incentive pass-through rate of 17%(83% enjoyed by firms) but only looked at the pass-through for the federal solar Investment Tax Credit(ITC), not for the CSI incentives. Henwood's(2014) best estimate[①] stated that only 36% of the CSI rebate was enjoyed by consumers(64% enjoyed by firms). Neither social demographics nor many PV system characteristics were controlled for in the analysis, however, and these omitted variables could confound the pass-through relationship if they are not equally distributed before and after the rebate-level changes. Wiser et al.(2007) estimated the impact of rebate levels on pre-

① Henwood(2014)also tried other model specifications, but the results were unstable.

rebate installed prices under an earlier PV rebate program in California, finding a coefficient of 0.56~0.73. Based on Eq. 13, the corresponding pass-through rate was 27%~44%. No time fixed effects(other than a linear monthly trend variable) were included to control for the seemingly positive correlation between rebate and price; additionally, because the work is somewhat dated, its results might not hold in the evolving solar market of today. Shrimali and Jenner(2013), meanwhile, studied 27 PV subsidy programs in 16 U.S. states over the period 1998—2009 and found that cash incentives were correlated with lower PV balance-of-system(BOS) costs(i.e., system price minus module cost). Similarly, Davidson and Steinberg(2014) claim that the decreasing CSI incentive drove down reported installation prices; however, PV incentives and prices could be automatically positively correlated, since they both decreased over time, and the causality could go in the other direction.

This research contributes to the broad pass-through literature by focusing on the largest state-level solar incentive programs in the United States: the CSI and, previously, the ERP. Our methods include both structural modeling and reduced-form regression analysis. I consider these two approaches to be complementary(Timmins and Schlenker, 2009). While the structural-modeling approach can better capture the equilibrium relationship and produce useful market competition results, the reduced-form analysis requires fewer structural assumptions and allows for more-flexible functional forms.[①] The combination of both approaches provides a test for the robustness of the pass-through results. Finally, as indicated earlier, in the next chapter I also use RD designs to take advantage of PV incentive step-down opportunities and geographic discontinuities in incentive levels between utilities. The current chapter complements those to-be-published RD results in terms of external validity.

3)Methods and Data

As mentioned above, I use both structural modeling and reduced-form

① The reduced-form analysis could potentially suffer from specification errors and omitted cost components bias, which can be avoided by assuming a constant pass-through rate. See MacKay et al.(2014) for more details.

regression analysis to estimate the pass-through rate for the CSI and the ERP. Because of its greater complexity, I focus in Section 4.3.1 on explaining the structural-modeling framework. In Section 4.3.2, I briefly discuss the regression specification for the reduced-form approach. Section 4.3.3 then summarizes the data used to conduct the analyses.

(1)Structural Modeling

The structural approach follows the established line of previous pass-through literature(Delipalla and Keen, 1992; Stern, 1987; Wolfram, 1999) and estimates a PV demand function, a supply relation, and the conduct parameter simultaneously. The pass-through rate can then be calculated from the parameters obtained through a predefined formula, together with appropriate confidence intervals.

Assume a market-level PV demand as:

$$Q=Q(P, X) \tag{14}$$

where P is the pre-incentive system installation price[①]($/W) and X is a vector of other control variables. Each installer i in the market is assumed to face the same demand and maximizes its own profits:

$$\max_{\{q_i\}} \pi_i = (\widetilde{P} + s)q_i - C(q_i, Z) \tag{15}$$

where $\widetilde{P}$ is the post-incentive price term(i.e., net price), s is the incentive(or subsidy)level($/W), q_i is the quantity produced by this installer, and C is the production cost, as a function of quantity and other factors Z.

Assuming installers compete in quantity, the first order condition of Eq. 15 is:

① Theoretically, the post-incentive system price(i.e., net price) should be used in the demand equation, since that is the price that PV consumers face. However, in my case, this is less important because the demand slope coefficients associated with either the price term or the net price term are almost the same, i.e., the incentive variable is roughly exogenous to the relationship between price and demand quantity. In addition, using the net price term creates a weak instrument problem if I use PV hardware cost as a supply shifter to instrument it, because the correlation between net price and PV hardware cost is very small. On the other hand, PV hardware cost is highly correlated with pre-incentive system prices, making it a very useful instrumental variable for the price term in the demand equation.

$$\widetilde{P} + s + \theta P_Q q_i = C_q \tag{16}$$

where $\theta = \dfrac{\partial Q}{\partial q_i}$ is the conduct(or market power) parameter that captures the responses of all firms when one installer changes its quantity.① The parameter θ nests various forms of imperfect competition(Weyl and Fabinger, 2013): $\theta = N$ refers to monopoly or tacit collusion with N as the number of installers in the market, $\theta = 0$ refers to perfect or Bertrand competition, and $\theta = 1$ refers to Cournot competition. Furthermore, P_Q and C_q are first derivatives of system price and product cost with respect to different quantity terms.

A market-level average of Eq. 16 can be derived as:

$$\widetilde{P} + s + \theta^* P_Q Q = C_Q = MC(Q, Z) \tag{17}$$

where $\theta^* = \dfrac{\theta}{N}$, and C_Q and $MC(Q, Z)$ are the market-level marginal cost.② The values of θ^* being equal to 1, 0, and $1/N$ correspond to monopoly, Bertrand competition, and Cournot competition, respectively; this is why $1/\theta^*$ is usually interpreted as the "equivalent number of firms" in the literature.

With this setup, I can then derive the incentive pass-through rate by taking the derivative of $\widetilde{P}$ with respect to s from Eq. 17. Following Delipalla and Keen(1992), the pass-through rate formula is as follows:

$$-\frac{d\widetilde{P}}{ds} = \frac{1}{1 + \theta^*(1 + A + E)} \tag{18}$$

where

$$A = -\frac{C_{QQ}}{\theta^* N \cdot P_Q} \text{ and } E = -P_{QQ}\frac{Q}{P_Q} \tag{19}$$

In other words, A is the relative slope of marginal costs to inverse demand(C_{QQ}/P_Q) along with the market conduct parameter θ^* and the number of installers N in the market. E is the elasticity of the slope of inverse demand.

---

① Unlike Wolfram(1999), I do not differentiate θ by installers in order to make the notations simpler; the pass-through formulas are still the same.

② This assumes q_i enters the marginal cost function linearly for each firm, which is reasonable since the first two moments of quantity in the production cost function are presumably the dominant ones, i.e., there is less need to consider third or fourth power here.

Following Wolfram(1999), Eq. 16 can be rewritten as the following supply-relation equation:

$$P = \widetilde{P} + s = MC(Q, Z) + \theta^* \frac{P}{\eta} \tag{20}$$

or furthermore as:

$$\theta^* = \eta \cdot \frac{P - MC(Q,Z)}{P} \tag{21}$$

where η is the absolute price elasticity of PV demand evaluated at the pre-incentive price P, i.e., $-\frac{1}{P_Q}\frac{P}{Q}$. That is why the conduct parameter θ^* is often called the elasticity-adjusted Lerner index. The rest of the problem is then how to obtain estimates for parameters in Eq. 18:(θ^*, A, E).

To add a more-specific context to the above derivation, below I specify the functional forms for PV demand and marginal cost and then develop the corresponding supply-relation equation. According to Bresnahan(1982), the identification of the above structural model requires at least one exogenous demand shifter that not only moves the intercept up and down, but also changes the demand slope. Therefore, I include both a price term and an interaction term between the system price and another exogenous variable.

In particular, the PV demand function is specified as follows:

$$\begin{aligned} Q_t = {} & \beta_0 + \beta_1 Q_{t-1} + \beta_2 P_t + \beta_3 (P \times Summer)_t + \beta_4 (Summer)_t + \beta_5 (TPO\_Ratio)_t \\ & + \beta_6 (\#\_of\_Zipcodes)_t + \beta_7 (\#\_of\_Installers)_t + \beta_8 (Fin\_Crisis)_t + \varepsilon_d \\ = {} & \beta_2 P_t + \beta_3 (P \times Summer)_t + \beta X_t + \varepsilon_d \end{aligned} \tag{22}$$

The measurement of all the variables is at the market level, which is defined here as each California county, following Davidson and Steinberg(2014). Time index t refers to a calendar month. Q_t is then the monthly market demand of installed capacity(in kW), Q_{t-1} is market demand in the previous month and indirectly captures many critical local-demand influences(e.g., household income, demographics, etc.), and P is pre-incentive installation price($/W). The interaction term between P and *summer* is to reflect that potential PV customers may respond to system price differently in different seasons,[①] where I define *summer* as an indicator variable for the second and the third quarters of a year(April to September). *TPO_Ratio* is the percentage of PV systems that are TPO, while *#_of_Zipcodes* and *#_of_Installes* are the number of zip codes and installers at time t in the market(i.e., in the county). *Fin_Crisis* denotes whether the system was installed in the financial crisis year of 2008. Lastly, ε_d is the error term. For the purpose of the remainder of this report and to simply the following equations, I further define X_t as including all variables other than the two price terms.

Furthermore, I specify the market-level(in this case, county-level) average marginal cost as:

$$MC_t = \delta_0 + \delta_1 Q_t + \delta_2 (Hardware\ Cost)_t + \delta_3 (Labor\ Cost)_t + \varepsilon_s \tag{23}$$

Eq. 23 can be considered the average of the installer-level marginal costs functions, since I only observe market-level hardware costs and labor costs. *Hardware Cost* includes both module cost and inverter cost, and *Labor Cost* is based on the annual wages of three professions related to the BOS costs: roofer, electrician, and administrative(Ardani et al., 2012). Further, the average of installer-level marginal costs is assumed to depend on monthly county-level PV installations(Q_t), captured by δ_1.

According to Wolfram(1999), the supply-relation equation in Eq. 17 can be characterized as follows:[②]

$$P_t = \frac{1}{1+\theta^*} MC_t + \frac{\theta^*}{1+\theta^*} h_t + \widetilde{\varepsilon_d} \tag{24}$$

where $h_t = \dfrac{\widehat{\beta} X_t}{-\widehat{Q_P}}$ with $\widehat{\beta} X_t$ and $\widehat{Q}_p$ defined in footnote 2. In other words, h_t

① As it turns out, it is important to include such an interaction term, as will become clearer in the discussion of model identification below.

② Missing steps from Eq. 17 to Eq. 24 are(omitting the error term): $P + \theta^* \frac{Q}{Q_P} = P + \theta^* \frac{\widehat{\beta_2} P_t + \widehat{\beta_3}(P \times Summer)_t + \widehat{\beta} X_t}{\widehat{\beta_2} + \widehat{\beta_3}(Summer)_t} = P + \theta^* P_t + \theta^* \frac{\widehat{\beta} X_t}{\widehat{Q_P}} = MC$, where parameters with hats are estimated coefficients. To further simplify, $P(1+\theta^*) + \theta^* \frac{\beta}{\widehat{Q_P}} X_t = MC \rightarrow P = \frac{1}{1+\theta^*} MC + \frac{\theta^*}{1+\theta^*} \left(\frac{\widehat{\beta} X_t}{-\widehat{Q_P}} \right)$.

is an imputed term from the estimation of Eq. 22. I then plug in terms from Eq. 23 for MC_t(suppressing the constant term), thereby addressing the problem that marginal cost is not directly observable.

$$P_t = \frac{\delta_1}{1+\theta^*} Q_t + \frac{\delta_2}{1+\theta^*} (HardwareCost)_t + \frac{\delta_3}{1+\theta^*} (LaborCost)_t + \frac{\theta^*}{1+\theta^*} h_t + \zeta_t \tag{24'}$$

θ^* can be easily recovered from the coefficient for h_t.① The two additional terms(*HardwareCost* and *LaborCost*) serve as supply shifters that are exogenous to the demand system, and they can instrument the price term in Eq. 22 since they can only impact demand through that price term. In the final estimation, I apply two-stage least squares(2SLS) to estimate Eq. 22 while only using *HardwareCost* as the instrument variable.② Similarly, the exogenous demand shifter$(Summer)_t$ not only identifies Q_t in the supply relation(Eq. 23), but also the conduct parameter ; see Bresnahan(1982) for more discussion. ζ_t is the new error term.

Bresnahan(1982) specified a slightly different version of Eq. 24' that used two quantity terms, Q_t and Q^*_t, where $Q_t^* = \frac{-Q_t}{\beta_2 + \beta_3 (Summer)_t}$; as a result, there is no need to impute h_t. To estimate the demand equation(Eq. 22) and this new supply relation(Eq. 24") simultaneously, there is no need to instrument the endogenous variable P_t and its interaction term,③ as in Wolfram's(1999) two-step approach. In the estimation process, I employed both approaches and found that their results are fairly similar.

$$P_t = \theta^* Q_t^* + \delta_0 + \delta_1 Q_t + \delta_2 (HardwareCost)_t + \delta_3 (LaborCosr)_t + \zeta_t \tag{24''}$$

---

① Assuming the coefficient for h_t is γ, then $\theta^* = \frac{\gamma}{1-\gamma}$.

② The *LaborCost* variable is not highly correlated with the price term, i.e., is not a good instrument to use.

③ This estimation approach, therefore, allows the use of the net price term instead of the price term in the demand model specification. I tested the use of net price, instead of price, finding that this choice produces nearly the same result. As such, to maintain consistency with the two-step estimation approach, I use the price term in the model results shown in this report.

As for the parameters(A, E) required to estimate the pass-through rate, after specifying a linear demand function—i.e., the price term enters Eq. 22 linearly—I implicitly assume E is equal to zero.[①] The only unknown C_{QQ} in A(Eq. 19) is δ_1 in Eq. 24' and Eq. 24'' if symmetric cost functions are assumed for all installers(Delipalla and Keen, 1992). After recovering A, market-level(i.e., county-level) pass-through rates can be estimated based on Eq. 18. The ultimate result of the structural modeling is therefore an estimation of distinct pass-through rates for each California county that is analyzed.

(2)Reduced-form Regression

As for the reduced-form approach, the regression analysis is conducted at the system level, with net price as the dependent variable. A large number of controls is included in order to account for the automatically positive correlation between system price and incentive level(see Figure 15 below) and to ensure that other important drivers of net price are controlled for, reducing the possibility of bias associated with omitted variables. Various fixed-effects models are applied.

The system-level, reduced-form regression used in the present study can be specified as follows:

$$(NetPrice)_{ijgt} = \beta_0 + \beta_1(Rebate)_{it} + \beta_2 X_{it} + \beta_3 Y_{jt} + \beta_4 Z_{gt} + \beta_5(Cost)_t + \varepsilon_{ijgt} \quad (25)$$

where indices i, j, g and t stand for a system, an installer, a zip code, and a time interval, respectively. The key independent variable is ***Rebate***, and its coefficient gives the pass-through rate. System-level characteristics X_{it} include nine variables: system size, system size squared, customer segment, TPO ownership, and whether the system uses China-manufactured modules, a micro-inverter, thin-film technology, building-integrated PV(BIPV), or tracking. Installer-level characteristics Y_{jt} contain two variables: the installer's cumulative installation experience through time t, and the installer density within the county per 10,000 households. Social-demographic variables at the zip code level Z_{gt} include household income, housing

① Including higher orders of price terms failed to pass the statistical significance test, so the estimate that E = 0 matches the data.

values, education levels, and total number of housing units within each zip code. *HardwareCost* and *LaborCost* from Eq. 23 are included via the cost term in Eq. 25. All price and cost terms were converted to real 2012 dollars. Finally, both zip code fixed effects and monthly fixed effects are assessed in this model, as part of the error term ε_{ijgt}.

In order to compare results with the structural-modeling approach and to explore county-level heterogeneity, I run Eq. 25 not only on the pooled full CSI/ERP dataset(described below), but also separately for each of the largest counties in California. As a result, statewide and county-specific pass-through rates are obtained through the reduced-form approach.

(3)Data

For variables in Eq. 22 and Eq. 23 of the structural modeling, I collected the majority of the data from the CSI but also used data from the ERP to extend the time series. The data I used were previously collected by LBNL as part of its Tracking the Sun(TTS)dataset.[①] I defined the market as a county—see Davidson and Steinberg(2014) for further discussion of this choice—and the time interval as a month based on the installation completion date, and I then calculated the averages of the variables at the county-month level. Specifically, I calculated monthly county-level PV installations as the total capacity of residential systems installed; estimated monthly county-level average prices, rebate levels, and net prices; and calculated the TPO ratio from the proportion of total TPO systems in the county-month. I simply summed the number of zip codes that had PV systems installed within the county-month as well as the number of active installers, also at a county-month

① The TTS dataset includes PV installation data collected from 47 PV incentive programs in 29 states. Those PV installation data were subsequently cleaned and standardized to remove potential errors in the data. The TTS series used here—TTS Ⅵ—includes reported PV system prices for more than 200,000 PV installations, representing 72% of cumulative grid-connected PV in the United States as of year-end 2012(Barbose et al., 2013). I use only that portion of the TTS dataset relevant to the current study: data from the CSI and ERP for residential PV installations in California, excluding appraised-value TPO systems.

level. I coded 2008 as the financial-crisis year. For the marginal-cost components, I calculated national average hardware costs by month from the TTS dataset, where reported(for both module and inverter costs). Lastly, I calculated a county-level weighted PV-related labor cost index using industry-specific raw data from the U.S. Bureau of Labor Statistics Quarterly Census of Employment and Wages,[①] deflated by the Consumer Price Index.

The reduced-form regression relies on the same data for both the CSI and ERP but supplements these data with other sources. System-level characteristics X_{it} were taken directly from the TTS dataset. As for the other control variables in Eq. 25, installer-level characteristics Y_{jt} were calculated from the TTS dataset. Specifically, I defined installer experience to account for all the installed capacity by the installer in the county but with an annual discount rate of 20% imposed on installations in previous years, and I defined installer density as the number of installers per 10,000 households within a county. Social-demographic variables Z_{gt} were collected from the Census(2000 and 2010) and the Census Bureau's American Community Survey(2005—2009, 2006—2010, and 2007—2011); missing values were estimated through interpolation.[②]

To clean and prepare the data, I only kept nominal system-level installation prices within \$1.5/W and \$20/W, and I limited system size to below 10kW(the vast majority of residential PV systems are expected to have prices and system sizes within these ranges). I only included PV systems installed between 2001 and 2012; data from earlier years were too sparse for effective use. Our analysis focuses on those 49 California counties with the longest PV installation history(i.e., having PV installations for more than 30 months). I dropped systems with rebate levels listed as zero or missing, and I dropped any system that used batteries, was self-installed,

① Specifically, I weighted roofer, electrician, and administrative wages using the ratio 2 : 1 : 2.5, which roughly corresponds to the relative amount of labor hours required from each type workerduring the installation of a typical PV system. I thank Kristen Ardani from NREL for providing these numbers.

② I thank Yale University for collecting, cleaning, and processing the social-demographic data.

or that reported a net price of negative or zero. By necessity, I excluded systems that could not be matched with the social-demographic variables. I also excluded systems installed in new home construction because of a high correlation with another independent variable(BIPV) in the monthly fixed-effects model. In cases with missing data for system characteristics, I imputed those characteristics where feasible; for instance, missing data for TPO can only be zero before 2007, since the TPO business model did not exist prior to 2007 for residential PV systems. Lastly, I excluded appraised-value TPO PV systems whenever using price or net price as the dependent variable, because reported appraised-value prices do not reasonably reflect actual installation costs.[①] These systems are, however, included in the demand equation(Eq. 22). Because of this approach, I only estimate pass-through rates for non-appraised-value PV systems in the results.

To showcase data for a few of the key variables used in the calculations, Figure 14 depicts residential PV installation and price trends for the ERP and CSI from 2001 through 2012. As shown,(pre-incentive) system prices have generally decreased with time, while system installation rates have increased. These two series are not very smooth, however, especially monthly installed capacity. Average residential system prices declined from 2001 to 2005, plateaued from 2006 to 2009, and then dropped rapidly through the end of 2012. Monthly installation rates oscillated considerably, with installations dipping owing to policy ambiguity before 2007(while the CSI was still being conceived) and during the financial crisis in 2008. Fluctuations in monthly installations also often link to rebate step changes, with a spike in rebate applications prior to step-downs in rebates(Henwood, 2014; Hughes and Podolefsky, 2013) and a subsequent reduction in applications for some period after rebates decline. Accordingly, a number of factors that influence demand for PV, and therefore system-installation trends, are reflected in Eq. 22. Finally, Figure 14 also presents a time series for module prices, which have moved closely with overall average installation prices—this is why module prices are included as hardware costs in the price equation(Eq. 23).

---

① See Barbose et al.(2013) for additional details on price reporting for TPO systems.

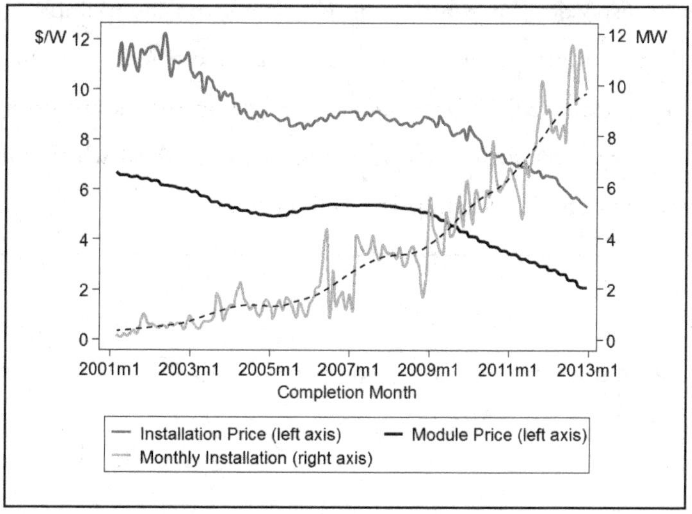

Figure 14 California Residential PV System Trends: Average(Pre-Incentive)System Installation Price, Module Price and Monthly Installation

Note: The dotted line is the smoothed curve of the monthly installation series.

Incentive pass-through can be illustrated by the relationship between(pre-incentive) installation prices and rebate levels. In Figure 15, such a relationship is drawn for one IOU in California, Pacific Gas & Electric Company(PG&E) under the CSI from 2007 to 2012, together with cumulative installed PV capacity. Both the installation prices and rebate levels are presented in nominal dollar terms, and all three variables are for residential PV systems only. The vertical dashed lines designate the step-down dates,[①] with the two circled step-down changes showing different relationships with installation prices. At the step-down just before 2009, for example, the pre-step and post-step installation prices appear to be largely constant. On the other hand, the rebate step-down in early April 2010 occurred in concert with a decline in installation prices. In other words, the first step-down appears to correspond to a complete pass-through rate, while the latter may suggest an incomplete pass-through(see Eq. 13 for more details). Estimating pass-through

① Knowing the exact step-down dates gives the CSI an advantage over the ERP, which is why Figure 15 does not extend earlier to the ERP.

rates by visual inspection, of course, is insufficient given the multiple confounding influences. For example, rebate levels and cumulative PV capacity have a strong negative correlation, while rebate levels and system prices are both positively correlated as time moves forward(also see Figure 14), both of which confound any simple correlation between system prices and rebates.

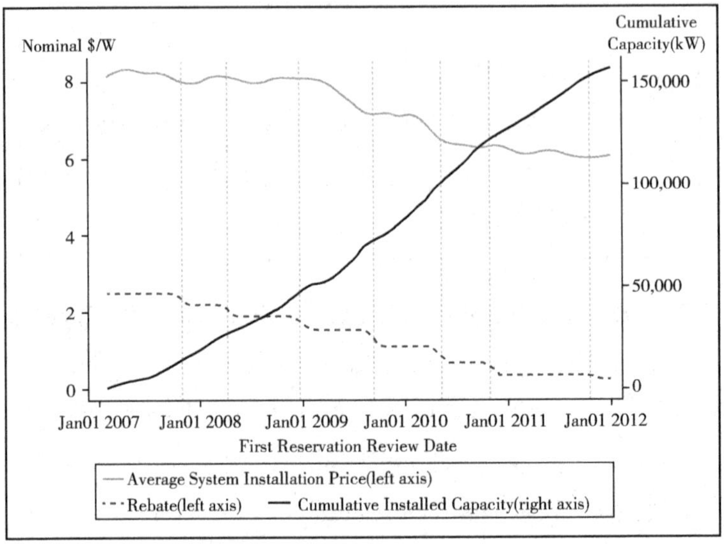

Figure 15 PG&E CSI Data: Residential Pre-Incentive Installation Price, Rebate, and Cumulative Capacity

Descriptive statistics are summarized in Table 6(at the county-month level) and Table 7(at the system level). Both only include data used for the later analysis—i.e., systems in the 49 counties with the longest PV installation history in California.

Table 6 County-level Summary Statistics for Structural Modeling: 2001—2012

Variables(County Level)	Mean	Std. Dev.	Min	Max	N
Installation price(real $/W)	8.50	1.94	2.71	21.48	5,677
Net price(real $/W)	6.19	1.23	0.20	18.24	5,677
Rebate(real $/W)	2.32	1.44	0.12	6.50	5,677
Monthly installation(kW)	80.36	150.3	0.58	1,799	5,677
TPO share	0.10	0.21	0	1	5,677

Continuation

Variables(County Level)	Mean	Std. Dev.	Min	Max	N
Summer season	0.50	0.50	0	1	5,677
# of zip codes	8.14	11.01	1	102	5,677
# of installers	6.92	8.89	1	69	5,677
Financial crisis year	0.09	0.29	0	1	5,677
Hardware cost(real $/W)	5.68	1.27	2.71	7.93	5,677
Labor cost(in $100,000)①	2.85	0.80	1.49	6.64	5,677

Table 7 System-level Summary Statistics for the Reduced-form Regression Analysis: 2001—2012

Variables(System Level)	Mean	Std. Dev.	Min	Max	N
Net price(real $/W)	6.211	1.865	2.4E−06	20.697	92,545
Installation Price(real $/W)	7.762	2.225	1.564	25.462	92,545
Rebate(real $/W)	1.551	1.304	0.074	8.825	92,545
System size(kW)	4.737	2.068	0.066	10	92,545
System size squared(kW^2)	26.715	22.046	0.004	100	92,545
Residential system	0.990	0.098	0	1	92,545
Commercial system	0.006	0.080	0	1	92,545
Other customer segment	0.003	0.057	0	1	92,545
TPO②	0.235	0.424	0	1	92,545
China module	0.175	0.380	0	1	92,545
Micro-inverter	0.142	0.349	0	1	92,545
Thin-film	0.026	0.160	0	1	92,545
Building-integrated(BIPV)	0.003	0.059	0	1	92,545

① Note that the labor cost is inflated because in the weighting mechanism, I multiplied the wage for roofer and administrative by 2 and 2.5 respectively.

Continuation

Variables(System Level)	Mean	Std. Dev.	Min	Max	N
Tracking system	0.001	0.025	0	1	92,545
Installer experience	0.325	4.475	0	195.84	92,545
Installer density	0.271	0.229	0	2.542	92,545
Hardware cost($/W)	4.876	1.302	2.709	7.933	92,545
Labor cost(in $100,000)	3.264	0.894	1.488	6.640	92,545
Household income(≤ $24,999)	0.160	0.080	0.007	0.695	92,545
Household income($25,000~$44,999)	0.155	0.058	0	0.581	92,545
Household income($45,000~$99,999)	0.325	0.067	0.049	0.587	92,545
Household income(≥ $100,000)	0.360	0.152	0.009	0.859	92,545
Housing value(≤ $34,999)	0.024	0.028	0	0.361	92,545
Housing value($35,000~$89,999)	0.039	0.052	0	0.663	92,545
Housing value($90,000~$249,999)	0.193	0.192	0	0.886	92,545
Housing value(≥ $250,000)	0.743	0.242	0	1.000	92,545
Less than high school	0.060	0.059	0	0.601	92,545
High school without diploma	0.064	0.041	0	0.365	92,545
Less than bachelor	0.495	0.130	0	0.835	92,545
Bachelor degree or more	0.381	0.182	0	0.912	92,545
Occupied housing units(in 10,000)	3.388	1.769	0.001	10.389	92,545

The data show several additional noteworthy features that impacted the model specification. First, PV deployment appears to grow not only from the installed base within the same zip code(Bollinger and Gillingham, 2012; Rai and Robinson, 2013), but also over time expands from one zip code to another within a county, suggesting both intra- and inter-zip code diffusion effects. This is, in part, why I included both a lagged demand term and the number of zip codes in Eq. 22.① Second, TPO market share increased over time. Under a TPO arrangement, a residential customer does not own the PV system, but instead hosts that system and purchases power from a third-party owner through a leasing or power-purchase agreement. In the reduced-form regression analysis, a TPO dummy variable was included, because TPO systems tended to show a slight price advantage relative to customer-owned systems, after excluding data for appraised-value systems. The growing attractiveness of TPO arrangements also needed to be controlled for in the demand equation of the structural modeling, as in Eq. 22.

4)Results

In this section, I present results for structural modeling and then for the reduced-form regression analysis. As described above, in the structural modeling, I adopted two approaches: one as in Wolfram(1999) that estimates Eq. 22 first using 2SLS and then estimates Eq. 24'(two-step estimation), and the other as proposed by Bresnahan(1982) that estimates Eq. 22 and Eq. 24'' at the same time(one-step estimation). I conducted these two analyses for each county. For brevity in presentation, I only show detailed regression results for one of the largest PV-installation counties(San Diego), but I also present summary statistics(median and standard deviation) for the regression coefficients of all 49 counties analyzed. Reduced-form regression results at the system level were produced for California as a whole, pooling data from all 49 counties considered. Additionally, for those California counties with sufficient PV data(150 data points or more), county-level pass-through results are presented.

(1)Structural Modeling

Focusing first on the structural modeling, Table 8 shows detailed regression

① To see the motivation more clearly, define q_{it} as the installed capacity within zip code i and Q_t as the quantity for the whole county. Then, $Q_t = \Sigma_i q_{it} = \Sigma_i(q_{it} - \bar{q}_t) + Z_t\bar{q}_t$, where $\bar{q}_t$ is the average installed capacity for all zip codes and is the number of zip codes, both at time . Assume is a linear function of $q_{i,t-1}$, thus, $Q_t = f(Q_{t-1}, Z_t)$.

results for San Diego county as well as summary statistics of the coefficients for all 49 counties in the analysis. These results are separated between the two-step estimation(Columns 1 and 2) and the one-step estimation(Columns 3 and 4). Results for the demand function are in Panel A, and results for the supply relation are in Panel B.

The first column of Panel A shows the regression results for PV demand in San Diego, based on the specification in Eq. 22(two-step estimation). With monthly installed capacity in kW as the dependent variable, I instrumented the price term with *Hardware Cost* and the price interaction term with a similar interaction term between *Hardware Cost* and *Summer*, as discussed earlier. Unit-root and co-integration tests were conducted to make sure the relationship in the time series analysis is stable. Coefficients for the lagged capacity and price terms have the expected signs and are statistically significant. Without instrumenting, these two coefficients will be slightly deflated, indicating a potential downward bias. The positive coefficient of the lagged capacity variable suggests a penetration effect(or peer effects at this high geographic level), consistent with previous literature(Bollinger and Gillingham, 2012; Dong and Rai, 2014). Moreover, price has a negative coefficient(even after being instrumented), indicating that consumers respond to lower price as would be expected, even after controlling for penetration effects. Using mean system price and monthly demand, I calculate a PV price elasticity of demand of 0.3 in San Diego, which is smaller than found by Zhang et al.(2011) but is consistent with the findings of Rogers(2014); the difference compared to Zhang et al.(2011) may result from the fact that penetration effects were not considered in that study.

The positive coefficient of the price interaction term with *Summer* indicates that PV consumers are less responsive to system prices during the two summer quarters. The negative coefficient for *Summer*, meanwhile, suggests that installations are lower in these months than in other months, all else being equal. As for other demand shifters, the prevalence of the TPO business model appears to attract more PV customer demand, consistent with Drury et al.(2012). As expected, the number of new markets in zip codes and number of installers in the market both contribute to higher PV adoption. Finally, the financial crisis is shown to have reduced PV demand in San Diego.

Looking across all 49 California counties in Column 2, qualitatively similar results are evident. Lagged capacity is found to be positively correlated with customer demand in 39 counties, while price is negatively correlated in 29 counties. For those counties with negative demand slope, the PV price elasticity of demand averages 0.6, with an absolute range of 0.08 to 1.9.① Results for the remaining variables were also broadly consistent with the results shown for San Diego, though with wide ranges in coefficient size due, in part, to differences in sample size.

Robustness tests were also done to control for other social-demographic variables, but those additional control variables did not change the main results, perhaps because they are largely captured already in the lagged capacity variable. I thus use the demand estimation results in Table 8 to impute the additional term($H = -\hat{\beta}X/\hat{Q}_P$) and inject it into the supply-relation regression for calculating the pass-through rate.

Table 8 Regression Output: PV Demand and Supply Relation for San Diego County and All Counties

	Two-Step Estimation		One-Step Estimation	
	San Diego	All Counties	San Diego	All Counties②
	(b/s.e.)	(median/s.d.)	(b/s.e.)	(median/s.d.)
Panel A: Demand				
Lagged Capacity	0.126*	0.106	0.153**	0.122
	(0.066)	(0.161)	(0.061)	(0.164)
Price	−21.745*	−0.564	−14.831***	−1.550
	(11.531)	(6.258)	(1.472)	(2.825)
Price × Summer	30.054**	0.812	33.707***	0.291
	(13.278)	(5.892)	(9.441)	(7.538)

① I did not differentiate the demand slope between summer quarters and other quarters when calculating demand elasticities. As with the San Diego results, I instrumented the price term with *Hardware Cost*.

Continuation

	Two-Step Estimation		One-Step Estimation	
	San Diego	All Counties	San Diego	All Counties②
	(b/s.e.)	(median/s.d.)	(b/s.e.)	(median/s.d.)
Summer	−286.707**	−5.911	−319.685***	−2.116
	(121.859)	(55.885)	(88.623)	(71.829)
TPO Ratio	501.526***	8.368	487.958***	12.359
	(103.138)	(98.899)	(94.209)	(110.914)
# of Zip Codes	9.823***	6.266	9.384***	6.395
	(1.236)	(3.093)	(1.167)	(2.393)
# of Installers	4.385***	3.622	4.890***	2.688
	(1.323)	(2.131)	(1.240)	(1.918)
Financial Crisis Year	−68.569***	−2.125	−55.427***	−2.656
	(17.121)	(13.880)	(16.906)	(14.320)
Panel B: Supply Relation				
Capacity(σ_1)	0.0007***	−0.0060	0.0014***	−0.0011
	(0.0003)	(0.0287)	(0.0003)	(0.0471)
Hardware Cost	1.211***	1.204	1.392***	1.169
	(0.117)	(0.258)	(0.110)	(0.295)
Labor Cost	−1.087	−0.159	−0.652	−0.158
	(0.718)	(1.150)	(0.687)	(0.989)
H Index(γ)	0.0010	0.0010		
	(0.0008)	(0.0301)		
Conduct Parameter(θ*)	0.0010	0.0010	0.0006	0.0004
	(0.0008)	(0.0333)	(0.0010)	(0.0134)
N	144	49	144	33

Note: Robust standard errors are in parentheses for the first and third columns, while standard deviations are in parentheses for the second and fourth columns; the constant term is suppressed; *p<0.10, **p<0.05, ***p<0.01.

Results for the supply-relation regression are shown in Column 1 in Panel B for San Diego, and in Column 2 for all 49 counties(two-step estimation). With the average system price as the dependent variable, the positive coefficient for capacity(installation scale in a month) suggests increasing prices with increasing market size in San Diego, all else being equal. Furthermore, hardware cost is passed through to installation prices, as would be expected. On the other hand, the increasing labor cost over time is negatively correlated with the simultaneously decreasing installation prices.

As for the imputed term H index, its coefficient can be roughly interpreted as the pricing response to the inverse of the absolute demand elasticity, and the small positive coefficient for San Diego means that lower demand elasticity tends to result in slightly higher prices. I then use the county-specific H index results to calculate the conduct parameter $\theta^*=\gamma/(1-\gamma)$ and the pass-through rate based on Eq. 18. The estimate of θ^* in San Diego is relatively small, resulting from the small coefficient for the H index. One way to interpret this result is that installers' pricing behavior did not significantly exploit the(relatively small) demand elasticity but instead responded to other more obvious factors such as hardware cost changes and penetration effects. A small or statistically insignificant conduct parameter also generally implies a high pass-through rate, as detailed later.

Looking across all 49 counties in Column 2, for at least half of them, the negative coefficient for the capacity term indicates returns to scale—higher installation scale is correlated with lower prices. Other coefficients in the supply relation tend to have a similar magnitude as in San Diego, except for the labor-cost variable. Importantly, as with San Diego, the median value for the conduct parameter is small.

Turning to the one-step estimation in Columns 3 and 4, here I applied the Full Information Maximum Likelihood(FIML) estimation technique.① Focusing first on the results for San Diego in Column 3, the one-step estimation coefficients are broadly consistent with the two-step results, but the generally smaller standard errors suggest greater estimation efficiency and precision. As with the two-step procedure,

① To implement FIML, I used the-nlsur-command in Stata with the-ifgnls-option; thanks to Kenneth Gillingham at Yale University for pointing us in this direction.

the conduct parameter is found to be very small. Results across all counties when using one-step estimation(Column 4) are similarly broadly consistent with the two-step estimation findings. The conduct parameter is found to be somewhat smaller than in the two-step estimation, and with a smaller standard deviation.

Figure 16 shows county-specific pass-through results from the two-step estimation approach only; results are very similar using the one-step estimation process. The pass-through rates vary from 92% to 103% depending on local market conditions(Figure 16a), generally with relatively narrow confidence bounds(Figure 16b). A pass-through rate of 100% indicates that, on average, ERP and CSI incentives and incentive changes were fully passed through to consumers, and it suggests sufficient competition among installers in such local markets. A pass-through rate of less than 100%, on the other hand, suggests weaker competition among installers and that installers did not set prices based solely on their marginal costs. Overall, I find that average county-level pass-through rates have been high(99%). For the 49 counties included in this structural-modeling analysis, only five have pass-through rates estimated at less than 95%.

A key reason for the relatively high pass-through rates is that the conduct parameters, as discussed earlier, are generally found to be small and close to zero.[①] The conduct parameters can also be inverted to obtain the numbers of "equivalent" firms[②] competing in the relevant PV market. For the 33 counties with positive conduct parameters, the median number of equivalent firms is 138, suggesting a reasonably high level of market competition. Nonetheless, in some counties only seven or eight equivalent firms have competed for customers, leading to somewhat lower pass-through rates.

① The conduct parameter coefficient remains small and close to zero even when I pool all of the counties together. This suggests that the small coefficient here is not due to small sample size.

② The number of equivalent firms is positively correlated with the actual number of firms across markets.

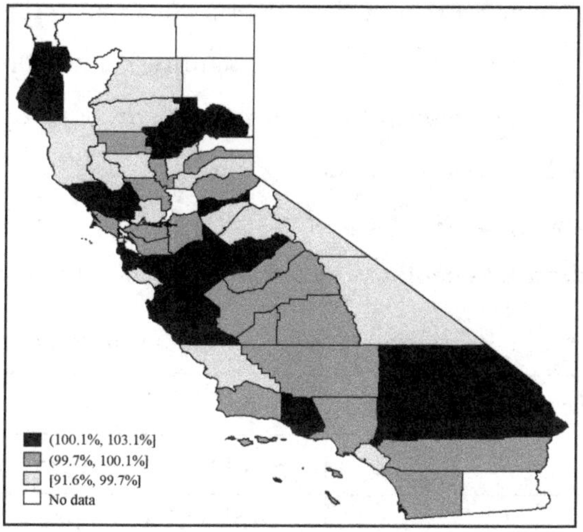

(a)Estimated Pass-through Rates

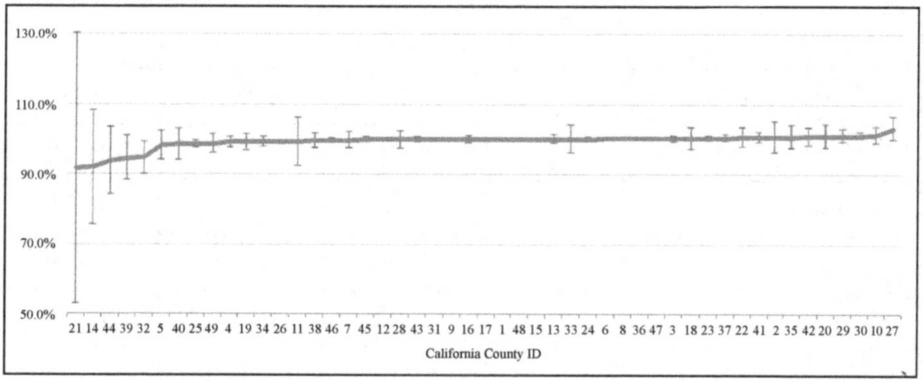

(b)95% Confidence Intervals for Pass-through Rates

Figure 16 Pass-through Rates for 49 California Counties: Structural-Modeling Approach

(2)Reduced–form Approach

As described in Section 4.3.2, the reduced-form approach consists of two versions of the same regression, both at the system level. One pools systems from all counties together, and the other is run for each county. I first show regression results for the all-counties case and then discuss the county-specific results.

Table 9 summarizes the regression results based on Eq. 25, with different sets of fixed effects added: M1 only contains zip code fixed effects, M2 only uses monthly fixed effects(and, accordingly, the hardware and labor cost terms are dropped, as these also are defined by time), and M3 includes zip code × month fixed effects. All models include social-demographic variables, the results of which are not presented here owing to space constraints, and all standard errors are clustered at the zip code level in order to account for series correlation in the error term.

Table 9 System-level Regression Results for 49 California Counties Together

Dependent variable: net price(real $/W)	M1	M2	M3
Rebate	-0.940^{***}	-0.855^{***}	-1.033^{***}
	(0.025)	(0.038)	(0.037)
System size	-0.942^{***}	-0.921^{***}	-0.950^{***}
	(0.035)	(0.033)	(0.050)
System size squared	0.066^{***}	0.064^{***}	0.066^{***}
	(0.003)	(0.003)	(0.004)
Commercial systems	0.038	0.096	0.133
	(0.099)	(0.099)	(0.196)
Other segments	0.735^{***}	0.706^{***}	0.760^{***}
	(0.133)	(0.133)	(0.267)
TPO	-0.323^{***}	-0.299^{***}	-0.267^{***}
	(0.029)	(0.036)	(0.044)
China module	-0.546^{***}	-0.532^{***}	-0.634^{***}
	(0.022)	(0.027)	(0.035)
Micro-inverter	0.458^{***}	0.516^{***}	0.476^{***}
	(0.032)	(0.035)	(0.053)
Thin-film	0.400^{***}	0.225^{***}	0.284^{***}
	(0.057)	(0.057)	(0.100)

Continuation

Dependent variable: net price(real $/W)	M1	M2	M3
Building-integrated PV(BIPV)	0.423***	0.384***	0.352
	(0.134)	(0.118)	(0.262)
Tracking system	1.288***	1.234***	1.640***
	(0.288)	(0.306)	(0.577)
Installer experience	−0.010***	−0.013***	−0.009*
	(0.003)	(0.003)	(0.006)
Installer density	−0.197**	−0.794***	0.156
	(853.9)	(661.5)	(4785.8)
Hardware cost	0.938***		
	(0.019)		
Labor cost	−0.151***		
	(0.033)		
Social-demographic variables	Yes	Yes	Yes
Zip code fixed effects	Yes		
Monthly fixed effects		Yes	
Zip code × month fixed effects			Yes
N	92,545	92,545	92,545
Adjusted R^2	0.322	0.297	0.464
Model degree of freedom	25	24	13

Note: Zip code clustered standard errors are in parentheses; *p<0.10, **p<0.05, ***p<0.01; social-demographic control variables are not reported owing to space constraints.

The key variable of interest is the rebate level, and the estimates show reasonably consistent results on the pass-through rate across all three reduced-form models, M1~M3, ranging from 86% to 103%. These average pass-through rates are also consistent with the results from the structural modeling, suggesting a relatively robust model specification. Based on the evaluation of the CSI/ERP programs, it would appear that rebates have largely been passed through to PV customers. Though not shown here, similar results are found when I limit the data sample to the CSI only or when I drop all TPO systems, not only appraised-value TPO systems. To be clear, because appraised-value TPO systems are necessarily excluded in all cases, the results cannot speak to pass-through rates among TPO systems broadly.[①]

Results for some of the control variables in Table 9 are also noteworthy. For example, hardware cost in M1 has a coefficient around 1, which suggests that hardware cost pass-through rates are almost complete. System size and its squared term have coefficients showing diminishing economies of scale with increasing system size, as one would expect. Non-appraised-value TPO systems may have some price advantage, relative to non-TPO systems. Systems with Chinese modules have relatively lower prices, as would be expected. Similarly, systems using micro-inverters, thin-film modules, trackers, or BIPV tend to have higher prices. On the other hand, installer experience reduces installation prices, presumably owing to within-firm learning-by-doing. Higher installer density also tends to correlate with lower installation prices.

The same system-level regression in Eq. 25 can be run for each county, thus forming an interesting comparison with the county-level structural-modeling results. Focusing only on the 42 counties with 150 or more PV installations, Figure 17 presents the pass-through results of this county-level analysis. In particular, the figure plots all pass-through estimates for M1~M3 that are found to be statistically significant, with t-statistics no smaller than 2.36. In total, statistically significant

① Non-appraised-value TPO systems report pricing based on transactions between installers and third-party owners, not between installers and end-use PV customers. As such, to the extent my results address pass-through for non-appraised-value TPO systems, it is the pass-through from the installer *to the third-party leasing company*(rather than to the actual host customer).

results are found for 36 counties in M1, 28 counties in M2, and 23 counties in M3. As shown, the overall results tend to center around a 100% pass-through rate, consistent with my previous estimates. In particular, the county-level weighted average(by the number of systems included in a county) pass-through rate is estimated at 95%. A more significant spread is found among counties, however, with pass-through rate estimates as low as 32% and as high as 270%, depending on the model. Some of this range may be due to limited sample size: focusing on the inner 10th~90th percentile of pass-through results, the range narrows to 68% to 122%.

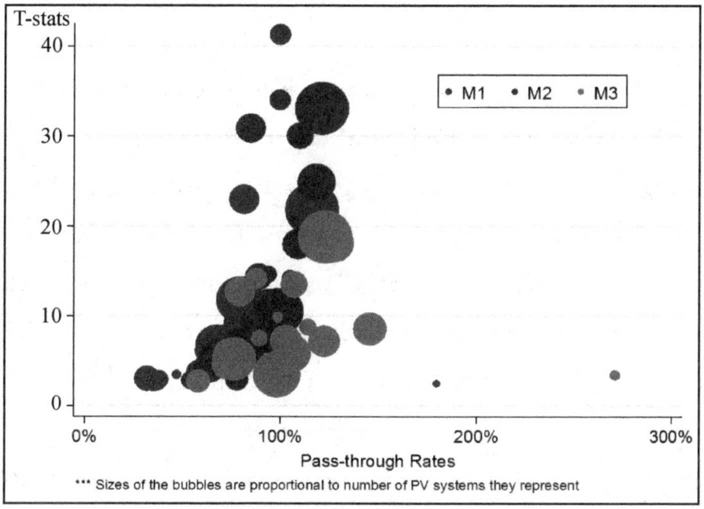

Figure 17 System-level Regression Results for County-specific Pass-through Rates

Note: Counties with less than 150 installed PV systems were excluded.

5)Conclusions

I find a high overall historical pass-through rate for the California residential PV rebate programs, though with some level of heterogeneity among counties. The structural-modeling approach estimates county-level pass-through rates that vary from 92% to 103%, with a mean value of 99%. The reduced-form regression analysis tends to find consistent results, with average pass-through rates ranging from 86% to 103% at the state level and with a county-level average pass-through rate of 95%. Focusing on the inner 10th~90th percentile of reduced-form pass-through results at the county level, a range of 68% to 122% is estimated. I consider these two approaches to be complementary: while the structural-modeling approach has a strong theoretical basis and can produce reliable results for relatively small markets, the reduced-form regression analysis is straightforward, easy to interpret, and does not require as many structural assumptions. Moreover, the next chapter that relies on RD designs similarly estimates high pass-through rates among the California solar incentive programs. The similarity of results from these various approaches to estimating pass-through rates lends credibility and robustness to those results.

In general, these results align with the qualitative observation that installers in California have tended to consider CSI and ERP rebates as exogenous factors when making pricing decisions, and they generally suggest a reasonably competitive market and a smoothly operating subsidy program. In part, these results may be due to the fact that California's rebate changes over time have been somewhat gradual, especially under the CSI, with each step-down representing a relatively small drop in the level of the state incentive. There may be little opportunity or motivation for installers to manipulate their pricing behavior in response to such small and somewhat-gradual rebate changes. These results may also suggest that installers have been competing more on quantity than on price, taking rebate step-downs as an opportunity to increase sales in advance of the step-down—a result consistent with that found in Gürtler and Sieg(2009) and Hughes and Podolefsky(2013).

Our high pass-through results stand in apparent contrast to those of other authors. Podolefsky(2013), for example, finds a rather low incentive pass-through rate for the federal ITC for residential PV. This lower estimated pass-through rate may be due to the relatively larger and more-abrupt changes in the federal incentive, over time, in comparison to the CSI. Similarly, Wiser et al.(2007) analyzed pass-through in California based solely on the earlier ERP, finding pass-through rates of well below 100%. In part this result may be due to suboptimal model specification.

In addition, the ERP experienced more-abrupt and sizable changes in incentive levels than the CSI, and it was in place when the solar market in California was less mature; this may help explain some of the discrepancy with the present results. Finally, my results appear to contrast with those presented in Henwood(2014). A key reason may be the different model specifications and different control variable sets: for example, though Henwood used utility-level fixed effects, I included zip code fixed effects; and while Henwood only controlled for TPO systems versus non-TPO systems, I included a large number of other system characteristics as important controls.

Though I find—using multiple methods—a high level of historical incentive pass-through in California, it is important to be careful in making broad claims based on these results. Our focus has been on residential PV systems in California, and I have excluded appraised-value TPO PV systems. As a result, the pass-through rates estimated here do not apply outside of California, and they do not apply fully to all TPO PV systems. Additionally, my results focus narrowly on the pass-through rate for direct solar incentives offered by the CSI and ERP. I do not evaluate so-called "value-based pricing" more broadly, which would necessarily consider the combined impact of direct state incentives, electric utility bill savings, and federal tax incentives.

Given these and other limitations, several additional areas of further research on incentive pass-through are warranted, both to assess the robustness of the present results and to judge their applicability in other market contexts. First, the reduced-form model results presented here may suffer from several forms of model bias. Use a RD design(as in next chapter) to judge PV system pricing across temporal or geographic boundaries may help improve the precision of the estimates of incentive pass-through rates. Second, though the present results focus entirely on California's PV incentive programs, other states have also developed a wide range of policy mechanisms to support solar market development. Assessments of incentive pass-through in markets outside of California—at the state and federal levels—would help improve the understanding of the robustness of the present results as well as the conditions under which pass-through rates are relatively higher or lower. Third, the current work focuses on the pass-through of California's CSI and ERP rebates, but PV customers benefit from PV through various other means as well, for example, the federal ITC, retail electric bill reductions, and sales of solar renewable energy certificates. As such, a more comprehensive evaluation of value-based pricing, considering all of these factors, is warranted. Finally, owing to data limitations, the analysis presented in this report focuses on customer-owned PV systems and non-appraised-value TPO systems. Further research is warranted to illuminate incentive pass-through and value-based pricing among all TPO systems, especially given the recent growth in the market for such systems.

Chapter 5 Analyzing Incentive Pass-through for the California Solar Initiative: A Regression Discontinuity Design

1)Introduction

Determining cause and effect is central to policy evaluation, and doing so requires that researchers construct counterfactuals(Heckman and Vytlacil, 2006). However, using observational data in empirical studies to determine cause and effect is challenging, with many threats to internal validity(Cook and Campell, 1979). This is the primary reason natural and quasi-experimental methods have become popular in the social sciences(Meyer, 1995; Shadish et al., 2001). For studies of solar energy incentive programs, a major cause-and-effect question revolves around the pass-through of incentives(also called subsidy pass-through, or subsidy incidence) to consumers: How much are the incentives passed through to consumers, thus encouraging them to buy solar systems rather than merely providing income to solar suppliers? Only a few studies have explored this question for the California Solar Initiative(CSI), the largest state-level incentive program in the United States(Dong et al., 2014; Henwood, 2014; Wiser et al., 2007). One explanation for this research gap is the difficulty of establishing a causal relationship using ordinary regression analysis. This chapter helps fill that gap by analyzing residential solar incentive pass-through for the CSI with a regression discontinuity(RD) design, a popular quasi-experimental method.

The CSI has a budget of more than $2 billion over a proposed program life of a decade(2007—2016). The rebate level has decreased in steps as capacity goals have been achieved(see Figure 1 and Table 2 for more details). The three biggest investor-owned-utilities(IOUs) in California administer this rebate program in their own territories with different capacity goals, and they have generally moved at different paces along the rebate ladders. These rebate variations provide good opportunities to analyze incentive pass-through with RD.

The incentive pass-through rate can be considered the marginal impact of incentive changes on the net(post-incentive) price paid by consumers. The pre-rebate price term also can be used as the dependent variable, but a transformation is required to obtain the pass-through rate. Per CSI statute, customers are entitled to the entire benefit of the subsidy. The actual amount of pass-through, however, might vary because PV installers likely change their pricing behaviors in response to subsidy changes. If an installer charges higher prices when incentives are larger, it absorbs part of the subsidy and reduces the incentive pass-through rate. On the other hand, if an installer lowers prices, the pass-through rate could become greater than 100%. Overall, CSI incentives act as a positive demand shifter, which could increase or decrease the supply costs depending on the marginal cost curve and thus change the market equilibrium price.

In the tax-incidence literature, the tax pass-through rate is determined by the relative curvature of demand and production cost curves as well as market competition(Delipalla and Keen, 1992; Fullerton and Metcalf, 2002; Sijm et al., 2012; Stern, 1987; Vivid Economics, 2007). Dong et al.(2014) followed this literature by adopting the conduct-parameter approach(Genesove and Mullin, 1998; Wolfram, 1999) and estimated a nearly 100% pass-through rate for two rebate programs in California: the Emerging Renewables Program(ERP, the predecessor of CSI) and CSI. Previously, Wiser et al.(2007) estimated the impact of rebate levels on pre-rebate installed price for the ERP and found a 27%~44% pass-through rate. One possible explanation for this discrepancy is the different periods covered in these two studies. While Dong et al.(2014) included only the period with a decreasing rebate to avoid the asymmetric pass-through effect(i.e., different pass-through rates for incentive increases and decreases; see Peltzman(2000) for a good review of this issue), the results from Wiser et al.(2007) might be driven by the large ERP rebate increase(from $3.0/W to $4.5/W) at the beginning of 2001.

The RD design in this chapter is used to explore the CSI's nine rebate step changes within each utility area(i.e., time discontinuities) and the geographic discontinuities between different utility areas. These discontinuities serve as natural experiments to tease out the causal effect of subsidy changes on the net PV price to consumers, which in turn identifies the pass-through rate. The RD design has been employed widely since the 1990s to study various issues, including the effect of class size on academic achievement(Angrist and Lavy, 1999), willingness to pay for good schools(Black, 1999), and incumbent advantages in elections(Lee et al., 2004), with its theoretical foundation laid out in Hahn et al.(2001). However, few studies have used RD designs to study the effect of solar incentives, especially the pass-through question. An RD design avoids the potential reduced-form biases highlighted by MacKay et al.(2014) by employing a non-parametric approach, thus improving the internal validity of the results.

This chapter makes three contributions to the literature on RD analysis and solar incentive pass-through. First, it focuses on the redistribution question of CSI directly and estimates the pass-through rate rigorously through causal effects. Although other studies have analyzed the CSI(Rogers, 2014; Hughes and Podolefsky, 2013; Peterman, 2012; Podolefsky, 2013; van Benthem et al., 2008), the incentive pass-through question has not been studied rigorously. Second, the simultaneous use of time and geographic discontinuities enhances the robustness of the results. Third, it combines RD designs with other methods—including difference-in-difference(DID), instrumental variables, and fixed effects—to solve potential bias problems caused by confounding factors when pooling multiple regression discontinuities together.

The rest of the chapter is organized as follows: Section 2 presents more information about the CSI and the opportunities to analyze it using RD analysis. Section 3 discusses the methods and data used. Section 4 presents the results of the analysis, and Section 5 offers conclusions.

2)CSI Policy Design and Suitability for RD Analysis

The CSI is the biggest state-level solar incentive program in the United States. To align the incentive level with the declining price of PV systems expected over time, the CSI designed a nine-step schedule to reduce the incentive level for all three IOUs, starting from 2007. For each step, the CSI has a capacity goal(in MW) for each IOU and customer segment and a corresponding rebate level(in $/W). Figure 18 shows the nine steps(Steps 2~10) on a calendar basis for each utility in the residential sector. The cutoff point between two incentive steps is based on the rebate reservation request review date, which is the date the program administrator receives the rebate reservation request and starts to review the application. When the application materials are complete and there is enough remaining capacity in the current step, the administrator assigns the applicant to the current step; otherwise the applicant is assigned to the next step. As Figure 18 shows, different IOUs have moved at different paces along the rebate ladder: Pacific Gas & Electric(PG&E) moved the fastest at the beginning, and San Diego Gas & Electric(SDG&E) caught up rapidly. Southern California Edison(SCE) lagged behind through 2012.

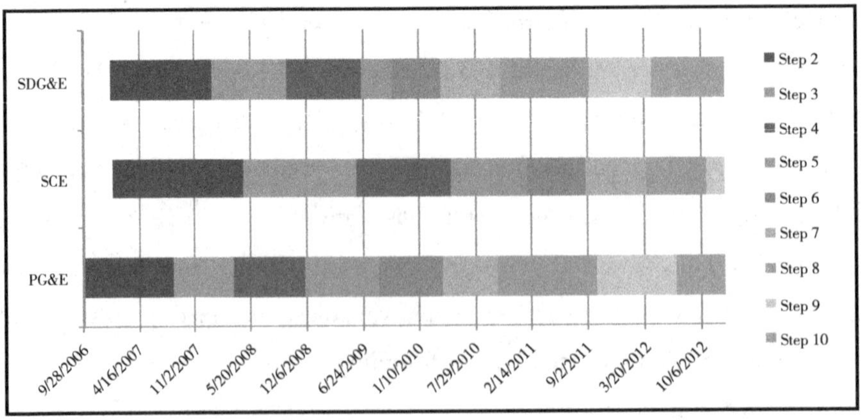

Figure 18 CSI Rebate Step Change Schedule by IOU

Each step change(or "stepdown") provides a unique opportunity to examine the impact of subsidy on the net consumer price paid, since it is reasonable to argue that PV systems reserved immediately before the stepdown are similar to those reserved immediately after it(at least with respect to system prices). On the other hand, reservations made before a certain cutoff date receive a higher rebate than those made after. This major difference highlights the key idea of RD: the exogenous discrete change in the incentive level offers a quasi-experimental opportunity to tease out the causal pass-through effect. Furthermore, the reservation request review date acts as the forcing variable, which determines the rebate level each PV system could receive.

One concern about the RD design is that the stepdown encourages more people to make a reservation immediately before the stepdown rather than after it, a phenomenon known as announcement effect(Gürtler and Sieg, 2009) or pulling-forward effect(Rogers, 2014). Hughes and Podolefsky(2013) considered this as evidence of consumers responding to rebate changes. As such, consumers who apply for the incentive immediately before the stepdown might be more price sensitive than those who apply after it(Henwood, 2014). If the pre-rebate installation price for the former group is relatively low compared to the price for the latter group, the pass-through rate could be higher than 100%; tests to account for this issue are described below.

The difference in PV-adoption speeds among California's utilities provides another interesting comparison. For instance, on August 17, 2007, PG&E moved to rebate Step 3 while SCE stayed at Step 2(Figure 18). This presents a great quasi-experimental opportunity within a small buffer area along the border of these two utilities' areas, using PG&E's stepdown in conjunction with SCE as a control group. Similar opportunities exist for other differential stepdowns among the three utilities(Figure 18). The underlying assumption is that residents on the two sides of the border between utility areas have similar demand for PV systems, and installers will not deliberately separate their markets based on utility borders. Even if constant and structural differences exist between two utilities, these can be accounted for through techniques like DID.

A key advantage of using RD to study the CSI is that all the stepdowns are predetermined by the policy, and the CSI administrator tracks the capacity-goal status and announces it publicly and frequently. In addition, the CSI discloses a dataset of the installed and reserved PV systems with installer names and installation prices. Such a policy design greatly reduces potential price manipulation by installers. Even the announcement effect might only shift the number of people around the stepdowns, and it has no significant impact on the installed price that customers pay. All of these factors suggest a relatively high pass-through rate, but additional analysis is required before making such a claim.

3)Methods and Data

A general introduction to RD can be found in Bloom(2012), Imbens and Lemieux(2008), Jacob and Zhu(2012), Lee and Lemieux(2010), and Wing and Cook(2013). In RD, the forcing variable is defined as the variable that causes a discontinuity(i.e., a jump) only in the key independent variable, but not in any other covariates. Consequently, if there is a similar jump in the dependent variable, a causal claim can be made with more confidence than when using other reduced-form regression analyses. As indicated above, the nine CSI stepdowns for each utility and the geographic border area between two neighboring utilities are suitable for the application of this method. Although over time some big installers can learn from the process and predict the stepdown dates closely, the RD design is still valid as long as there are inherent uncertainties to installers' predictions. According to Lee and Lemieux(2010), imprecise control over the forcing variable is sufficient to generate random assignment around the cutoff point. Furthermore, density tests can be done to examine if the forcing variable has been manipulated(McCrary, 2008). In addition, in this chapter, a geographic discontinuity is employed to complement the time discontinuity.

(1)Methods

For the RD time discontinuity, the reservation request review date is the forcing variable, denoted by x. Within a certain window around the cutoff date,

x_0(when the stepdown occurs), the rebate steps(r) that each PV system falls into can be determined as follows:

$$r = \begin{cases} i & \forall x \in [x_0 - h, x_0) \\ i+1 & \forall x \in [x_0, x_0 + h) \end{cases} \tag{26}$$

where the window size is h, measured in number of days, and i is the step number(2 to 9). In general, researchers redefine x_0 to be zero by deducting x_0 from each x. Thus, all x's to the left of the cutoff point become negative, and those to the right become positive. Negative x's correspond to the rebate step r_i, and nonnegative x's correspond to the next step, r_{i+1}. Such mapping from the reservation request review dates to the rebate steps forms a sharp RD design, because there is no possibility of a nonnegative review date corresponding to the previous rebate step(r_i instead of r_{i+1}) or a negative review date for the next rebate step(r_{i+1} instead of r_i). Furthermore, a few crossovers① through cutoff points make the design a fuzzy RD, but it is still identifiable in a similar way as the sharp RD(Battisti and Rettore, 2008). Rebate steps can be linked further to rebate levels using the information in Table 9. Next, the change in net price($NP = P - s$, where P is the pre-rebate price and s is the rebate), in response to rebate reductions after x_0(now zero) is used to estimate the pass-through rate.

In the case of geographic discontinuity, the forcing variable is the distance to the common border between two neighboring utility areas(d_i).② Only a relatively small buffer area away from the border(e.g., 10 miles) is examined. Essentially, the choice of the size of the buffer zone is a tradeoff between data availability and potential biases, which can be experimented with. In this geographic setting, systems in one utility area have a distance in negative numbers(minus 0~10 miles), and

① Crossovers in this context refer to the cases where PV customers receive different rebate levels from what is determined by the forcing variable, i.e. the reservation request review date. For example, on August 16th, 2007 in the PG&E area, the rebate level should be \$2.5/W at Step 2, but some customers may have already been assigned to Step 3 and only got \$2.2/W instead.

② As in Dell(2010), the latitude and the longitude can instead be used together as the two-dimensional forcing variables, but her results indicate that using distance produced the same results.

systems in the other area have a distance in nonnegative numbers(0~10 miles). The sign of this forcing variable also will correspond to two different rebate rates for similar PV systems during a certain period. However, in this case, caution must be exercised about the preexisting differences between the two utility areas, which can confound the rebate rate differences.

One of the key assumptions to estimate the pass-through rate using RD is the unconfoundedness assumption, i.e., $NP \perp s \mid x$(Rosenbaum and Rubin, 1983): conditional on the forcing variable, the dependent variable is orthogonal to the key independent variable. In other words, the incentive level is totally determined by the forcing variable. This assumption, along with the continuity assumption, enhance the internal validity of the RD designs so that such designs are similar to random, controlled experiments(Imbens and Lemieux, 2008; Lee, 2008), while the continuity assumption requires that the distributions of the dependent variable and other unobserved control variables be continuous around the cutoff points in the forcing variable.

In order to obtain estimates in RD, there are complementary parametric and non-parametric ways to run the regression(Lee and Lemieux, 2010). Following the literature, the parametric model is specified here as follows:

$$NP_i = \beta_1 \cdot s_i + f(x_i) + f(x_i) \cdot D_i + \varepsilon_i \qquad (27)$$

where s_i is the rebate level a PV system i receives, and D_i is the dummy variable indicating if the rebate step is at a higher level or not. $f(x_i)$ is a flexible functional form of the forcing variable x_i to control for continuous changes from other confounding factors around the cutoff point(Angrist and Pischke, 2009). Researchers often characterize it as a polynomial with different orders. The interaction term $f(x_i) \cdot D_i$ further allows the continuous changes of other variables to differ from one side of the cutoff point to the other. Because of this parametric specification, β_1 gives the pass-through rate.①

---

① In a sharp RD design, Eq. 27 is equivalent to $NP_i = \beta_1 \cdot s_i + f(x_i) + f(x_i) \cdot D_i + \varepsilon_i$; however, the advantage of Eq. 27 is that it estimates the pass-through rate directly, whereas the equivalent form has to divide the estimated $\hat{\beta}_1$ by the actual rebate rate changes around the cutoff point. The same principle applies to Eq. 28.

The non-parametric approach can be approximated by a local linear regression with different kernel options and with a relatively small bandwidth(or window) around the cutoff point. The bandwidth is optimally chosen considering the tradeoff between bias and efficiency. Assuming the optimal bandwidth is ω, the non-parametric approach specifies the local linear regression as follows:

$$NP_i = \beta_1 \cdot s_i + \beta_2 \cdot x_i + \beta_3 \cdot (s_i x_i) + u_i \quad \forall i \in (x_0 - \omega, x_0 + \omega) \tag{28}$$

where β_1 again gives the pass-through rate, as it captures the jump in the dependent variable at the cutoff point, after controlling for other potential confounding factors through the two terms. Usually, the parametric model in Eq. 27 should also be estimated within an appropriate window around the cutoff point, which is generally larger than that of the nonparametric model in Eq. 28. Nonetheless, what Eq. 27 and Eq. 28 are able to capture is the same, the so-called local average treatment effect(LATE). Generalizing the results beyond the window requires stronger assumptions and might be problematic. In addition, for both approaches, other control variables can be added; however, if RD works, doing so should not impact the results in the coefficients obtained.

In the case of CSI pass-through, if all the stepdowns were pooled within one utility together and the regression run in either Eq. 27 or Eq. 28, the trend issue becomes a new concern(Ito, 2013), i.e., both the net price and the rebate tend to decrease over time(even within the window periods included in the regression for one stepdown). On the other hand, if two utilities were pooled together and the border areas between them compared as in the geographic discontinuity case, one utility must form a compatible control group, and the difference between the control group and treatment group must only be caused by the stepdown. This is discussed further in Section 5.4.

The recent development of RD designs has taken multiple directions. For example, Imbens and Kalyanaraman(2012) develop nonparametric methods to select the RD bandwidth optimally. Calonico et al.(2014) propose robust confidence intervals for various RD designs. Angrist and Rokkanen(2012) discuss RD identification away from the cutoff. Dell(2010) and Reardon and Robinson(2010) discuss the application of two or more forcing variables. Grembi et al.(2013) and Ito(2013) combine the DID technique with RD. At the same time, the number of empirical studies with RD applications is growing exponentially. The key message is that the RD framework might need to be adapted to the specific research question and combined with other techniques such as fixed effects and instrument variables(IVs).

(2)Data

The data requirement for RD designs is very limited if there are no tests on the underlying assumptions and robustness checks. To implement the time discontinuity, small windows are zoomed into around the rebate stepdowns, and the impact of rebate changes on the net price is examined within one utility. To explore the geographic discontinuity, two utilities must be compared at one time where systems installed on different sides of the buffer zone are similar to each other except for their rebate rates. For each of the RD designs, three variables are of most importance: the dependent variable(net price), the key independent variable(rebate rate), and the forcing variable(either the reservation request review date or the distance to the utilities' shared border). In addition, more variables are needed to test the RD assumptions and robustness.

This study leverages the Tracking the Sun database collected by Lawrence Berkeley National Laboratory(Barbose et al., 2013). The major advantage of this dataset is the physical street addresses for almost all installed PV systems in California, which enables the calculation of distances to shared borders. Only the CSI dataset is examined here, since the rebate-adjustment process in ERP is less known and thus inappropriate for use with RD designs. Other than the three key variables within an RD design, PV system-level characteristics and other social-demographic variables from the Census were used to test if these variables are balanced before and after the stepdowns. This precondition for RD designs ensures that there is no discrete change in any of the confounding variables around the cutoff point. System characteristics include system size, ownership model(third-party owned or not), China-manufactured modules or not, micro-inverter or not, thin-film modules or not, and building-integrated PV or not. Census data include household income levels, owner-occupied housing values, household education levels, and total population in occupied housing units at the zip code level.

To show data used for the time RD approach, Figure 19 depicts a 2-week window around the reservation request review date when PG&E moved from rebate Step 2($2.5/W) to Step 3($2.2/W) on August 17, 2007. Three curves are shown, representing daily averages: system price, system net price, and rebate level. When system price decreased by about $0.3/W from August 16 to 17, the reduction of the rebate(also $0.3/W) offset that trend and flattened out the net-price curve. This suggests a pass-through rate of about 100% within this neighborhood. One particular concern here is the possibility of reverse causality, i.e., that the system price dropped because the rebate level was reduced, assuming the system price drop was strategically determined by installers. In that case, the corresponding pass-through rate would be much less than 100%, since a complete pass-through requires that the system price not change before and after the stepdown; with a reduced post-stepdown price, the corresponding pass-through rate is less than complete. Though installers are likely to lower their prices in response to rebate reductions, in some cases system prices have a temporarily increasing trend before the stepdown. Furthermore, it is difficult to imagine almost all installers coordinating to lower their installation prices at the same time and just for one day and then increasing their prices again. An exogenous reason for the price change is much more likely.

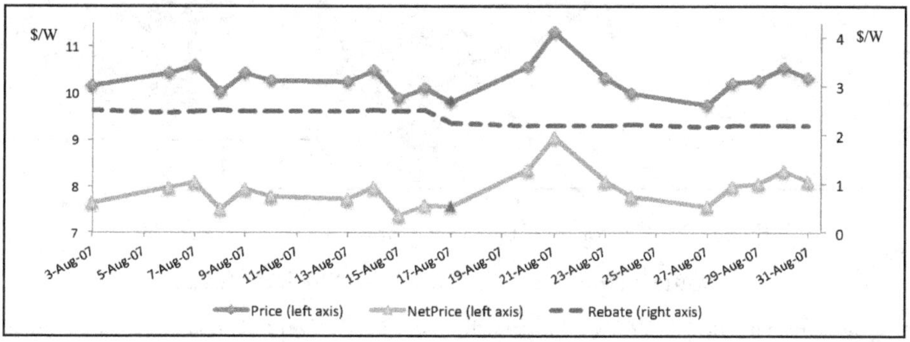

Figure 19 Example of CSI Time RD Opportunity: PG&E Rebate Stepdown 2~3

As to the geographic RD approach, Figure 20 shows the physical addresses of installed PV systems on a GIS map, with information on the boundaries between utility areas provided by Ventyx. The figure shows a 5-mile buffer zone on both sides of the utility boundaries. Although the boundary between PG&E and SCE is long in the north, much of the corridor is in rural and mountainous areas. In the south, the buffer zone between SCE and SDG&E has more PV installations owing to its high population density. This phenomenon remains if the buffer zone is expanded to 10 or 20 miles. In addition, the PV systems seem to be located roughly symmetrically across the utility boundaries, which should improve the likelihood

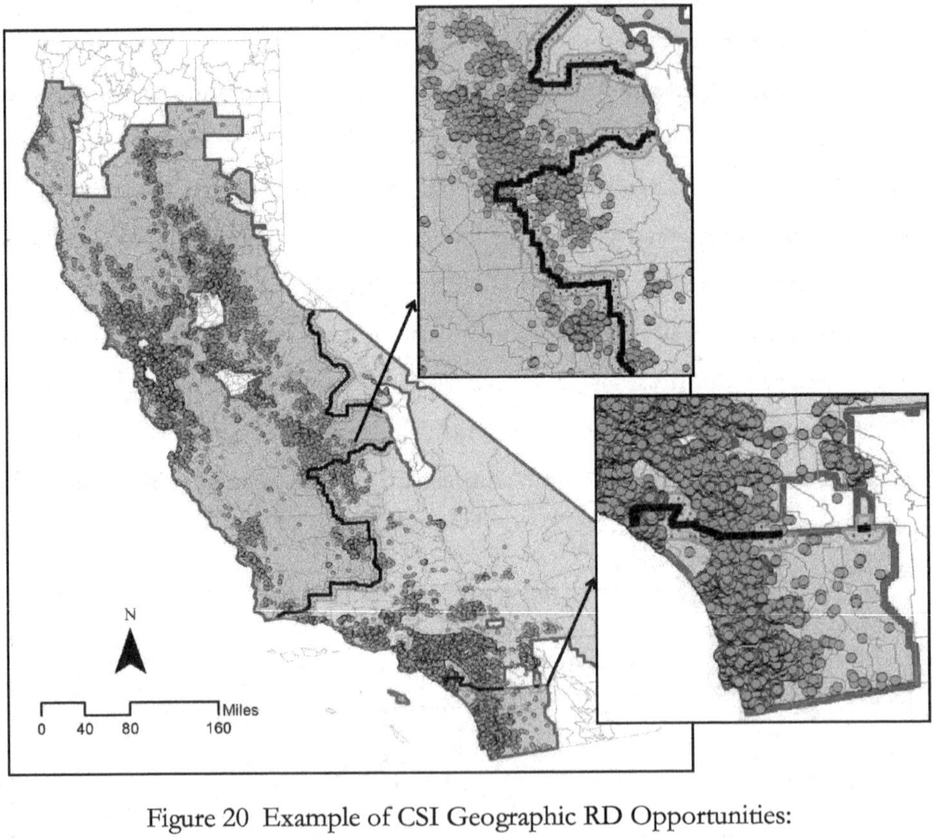

Figure 20 Example of CSI Geographic RD Opportunities: Borders among PG&E, SCE, and SDG&E Areas

Note: Green dots are actual PV addresses, light polygons are zip code boundaries, and 5-mile buffer zones are shown in yellow areas(with orange lines) on both sides of the utility boundary.

that these systems are from the same zip codes and thus improve the credibility of the geographic RD designs. Using the 5-mile buffer, about 40% of the systems share the same zip codes across the north boundary, whereas 53% of them do so in the south.①

To compare the buffer area between two utilities, either the whole time series from 2007 to 2012 can be analyzed, or a small window can be examined when one utility experienced a stepdown while the other did not within a certain period. The latter approach is similar to what this study does for the time RD case but for two utilities at the same time. It is more reliable than the former approach simply because it avoids the impact of potential confounding factors that change in a relatively longer cycle than the chosen window. For example, in the long run, if one utility changed its rate structure while the other did not, this could confound the relationship between rebate rate and net price. In addition, both utilities have experienced stepdowns over the long run, thus it is more difficult to isolate the impact of rebate level changes on the net price. To avoid such difficulties, this study focuses on several time windows across the boundaries based on Figure 18. Three stepdowns by PG&E and four stepdowns by SDG&E are identified, and SCE serves as the control group in both cases.②

Summary statistics are necessary to see if the control group is valid in the DID comparison, and they give insight into the potential pass-through rate. Figure 21(a) summarizes the system price changes for the three chosen PG&E stepdowns when there was no simultaneous stepdown for SCE. As the figure shows, SCE is a perfect control group because there are almost no SCE price changes before and after PG&E's stepdowns. Although the PG&E price increased during stepdown 2~3 and decreased during stepdown 7~8, none of these changes are significantly different

① It is ideal but not necessary for PV systems to share the same zip codes on both sides of the utility boundary, since other zip codes can still be similar to each other.

② The major selection standard used here is that, starting from the cutoff date in the utility with a stepdown, the timeline of the other utility can be traversed forward and backward for at least 3 months(90 days) without hitting a stepdown.

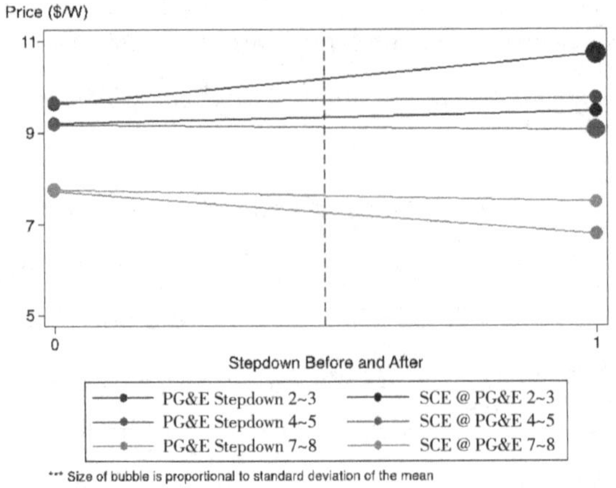

(a) PG&E vs. SCE

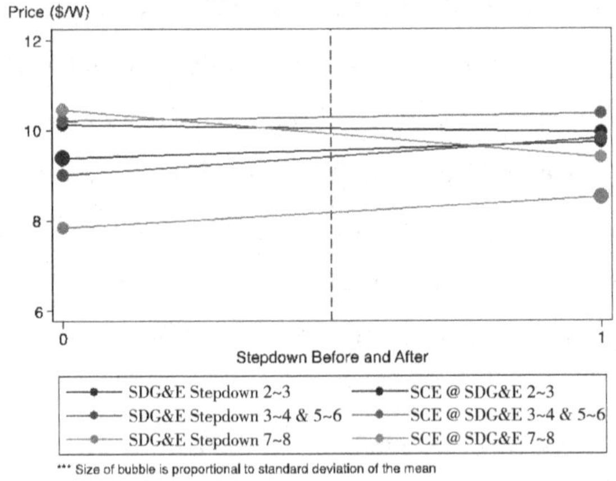

(b) SDG&E vs. SCE

Figure 21 Price Changes around Stepdowns for the Treatment Group and the Control Group

Note: A 60-day time window is used for all the stepdowns, each bubble in the graph represents an average of 60 days, and in panel(b)SDG&E stepdowns 3~4 and 5~6 were combined to reduce the number of lines.

from zero. On average, for these three stepdowns, the pre-rebate price remained relatively constant before and after the step changes. Seemingly, the corresponding pass-through is close to 100%. Comparing between SDG&E and SCE in Figure 21(b) shows a similar picture but with some difficulties. By testing the difference(of two utilities) in the difference(before and after stepdowns) term of the installation price, the(pooled) price change between these two utilities is significantly different from zero. The problem lies in the large price decrease experienced by SCE when SDG&E went through stepdown 7~8, which failed the control group requirement. As a result, running a DID regression or the RD approach will generate upward-biased results, and modifications are required.

Another methodological concern is that, when PG&E experienced stepdown 4~5, SCE stayed at Step 3 for the whole time. Ideally, SCE would stay at step 4 during this period, so SCE and PG&E have the same rebate at the beginning; instead, there are net price differences between the two utilities even before one has a stepdown. The consequence is a downward-biased pass-through rate if RD is applied directly. The same situation applies to the comparison between SDG&E and SCE. This bias and the bias from the unwanted control group price reduction are formalized below.

Figure 22 captures the two cases of potential bias for the DID comparison: panel(a) is the ideal case, while panel(b) is the actual case. In panel(a), both SDG&E(which also could be replaced with PG&E for this illustration) and SCE start from the same rebate step($R0 = R1$) and have the same net price($NP0 = NP1$) before the SDG&E stepdown. Then, only SDG&E experiences the stepdown, and the rebate rate decreases to $R1'$. If the pass-through is complete, the net price in SDG&E will increase by the amount of the rebate reduction. In other words, the extent that $NP1$ increases to $NP1'$(relative to the extent $R1$ decreases to $R1'$) determines the pass-through rate in this ideal case. On the other hand, in panel(b), there are two differences from the ideal case: 1)the control group—SCE—experiences a price decrease($NP0' - NP0 < 0$) during SDG&E's stepdown(i.e., the upward bias), and 2)the starting rebate rate in SDG&E is lower than that in SCE($R1 - R0 < 0$), so the net price in SDG&E before the stepdown is greater($NP1 - NP0 > 0$)(i.e., the downward bias).

The pass-through rate is then calculated in the following way. The baseline is defined as the initial pass-through rate using only data observed before the stepdown:

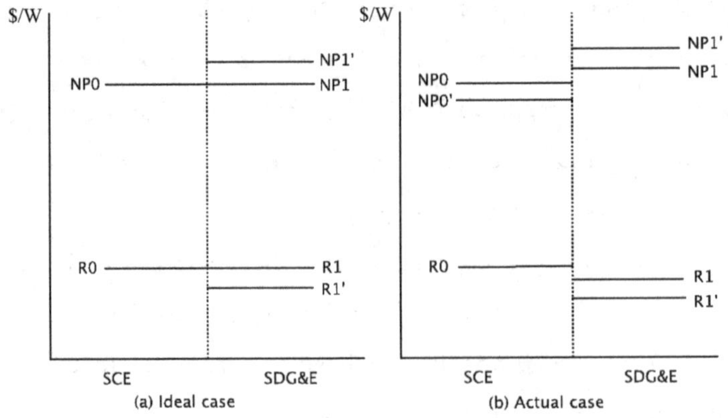

Figure 22 DID Comparison in Geographic Discontinuity: Ideal and Actual Cases

$$PT_0 = \frac{NP1 - NP0}{R1 - R0} \tag{29}$$

PT_0 is obviously zero in the ideal case. After the stepdown, $NP1'$ and $R1'$ are observed, so the pass-through rate then is:

$$PT_1 = \frac{NP1' - NP0}{R1' - R0} \tag{30}$$

The true pass-through rate for the ideal case is the difference between these two pass-through rates:

$$PT^* = PT_1 - PT_0 = PT_1 = \frac{NP1' - NP0}{R1' - R0} = \frac{NP1 - NP0 + \Delta NP}{R1 - R0 + \Delta R} = \frac{\Delta NP}{\Delta R} \tag{31}$$

Eq. 31 usually takes a negative sign, and a more intuitive complete pass-through rate corresponds to the absolute value of Eq. 31, which is then multiplied by 100%.

Now the two key differences between the ideal case and the actual case are introduced as in Figure 22(b). PT_0 takes the same form but now becomes negative(likely greater than −1). Also, the net price in the control group decreases from $NP0$ to $NP0'$ now. PT_1 is then slightly different:

$$PT_1 = \frac{NP1' - NP0'}{R1' - R0} \tag{30'}$$

Consequently, the pass-through rate is changed to:

$$PT^{*} = PT_1 - PT_0 = \frac{NP1' - NP0'}{R1' - R0} - \frac{NP1 - NP0}{R1 - R0} \tag{31'}$$

Through some algebra, Eq.(6′) can be simplified to:

$$PT^{*} = -\underbrace{\frac{\Delta R(1 + PH_0)}{\Delta R + R1 - R0}}_{\text{Initial condition bias}} + \underbrace{\frac{NP0 - NP0'}{R1' - R0}}_{\text{Control group bias}} = -\frac{\Delta R\uparrow}{\Delta R\downarrow} + \frac{(>0)}{(<0)} \tag{32}$$

As a result, when the two utilities failed to start from the same rebate level, this caused a downward bias in the pass-through rate, i.e., the initial condition bias. The bias is downward because, without such bias, $PT^{*} = -\frac{\Delta R}{\Delta R} = -1$, as assumed in the middle of the calculation, and the corresponding pass-through rate is 100%; with this bias, the numerator is biased upward(i.e., less negative), while the denominator is biased downward(i.e., more negative), and the resulting pass-through rate is smaller than 100%. On the other hand, when the control group also experienced a price decrease in the same period, this caused an upward bias, i.e., the control group bias. Such bias is caused by the price decrease in the control group($NP0 - NP0'$), adding a very negative term to the PT^{*} expression and thus inflating the true pass-through rate greatly.①

The above deduction is essentially the idea of difference-in-RD(Grembi et al., 2013), where a geographic RD regression is run before and after the stepdown for two different utilities separately, and then the difference between their estimated pass-through rates is taken. This approach is better than a simple geographic RD design that compares two neighboring utilities but only examines the post-stepdown period. Unfortunately, it only works in the ideal situation as demonstrated above; when there are confounding sources, as described above, the results can be biased either way.

Now the simple RD design must be adapted to account for the potential biases. For the initial condition bias, the solution is either to run the regression for the treatment group as done for the time RD approach or to isolate the variation

① The second bias is not a problem when comparing PG&E and SCE, based on Figure 21(a).

in the rebate rate variable and use it to identify the corresponding response in the net price term. The second method is preferred, because it avoids repeating the time RD analysis. The modification focuses on the variation in rebates from $R1$ to $R1'$, but not from $R0$ to $R1'$, since the part from $R0$ to $R1$ is the source of the initial condition bias(the variation is supposed to be zero in the ideal case). The variation can be isolated using the interaction term between the utility dummy variable and the stepdown dummy to instrument the rebate rate variable. For the control group bias, more control variables can be introduced to explain the unexpected price decrease in the control group, which seems to be equivalent to instrumenting the rebate rate variable with more variables than the interaction term(including these new control variables).

4)Results

In the following, the RD results for the time discontinuity are presented first, followed by the results for the geographic discontinuity. Other results for assumption tests and robustness checks are presented together when necessary.

(1)Time Discontinuity

As mentioned in Section 5.3.1, there are parametric ways and nonparametric ways to run the time RD regression for each utility. Also, the regression can be run for each stepdown separately, or the stepdowns for each utility can be pooled together. The results for PG&E are presented below as an example, followed by highlights of results for the other two utilities.

①Parametric Model for Time Discontinuity

Using Eq. 27, different orders of polynomials(one to four) of the forcing variable are fit to control for any continuous changes on both sides of the stepdown and to ensure the functional form will not drive the results. For example,using a cubic control function, Eq. 27 can be rewritten as:

$$NP_i = \beta_1 \cdot s_i + x_i + x_i^2 + x_i^3 + x_i D_i + x_i^2 D_i + x_i^3 D_i + \varepsilon_i \qquad (27')$$

Figure 23 displays the results for the parametric RD approach when a cubic polynomial is fit for the reservation request review date separately for both sides of

PG&E stepdown 2~3. Note that the reservation request review date is constrained to be within 35 days(or five weeks) of the stepdown date, to strike a balance between introducing too much bias and having a sufficient sample size.① As a result, the estimated coefficient is −1.042, indicating an almost 100% pass-through rate.② This corresponds to roughly a \$0.3/W increase in the net price, which is also the size of the reduction in rebate level. However, owing to random noise seen in Figure 23, the pass-through rate is statistically insignificant. Fortunately, PG&E has nine steps and eight stepdowns to explore. By pooling all these stepdowns together, the larger sample size helps estimate the pass-through rate more precisely.

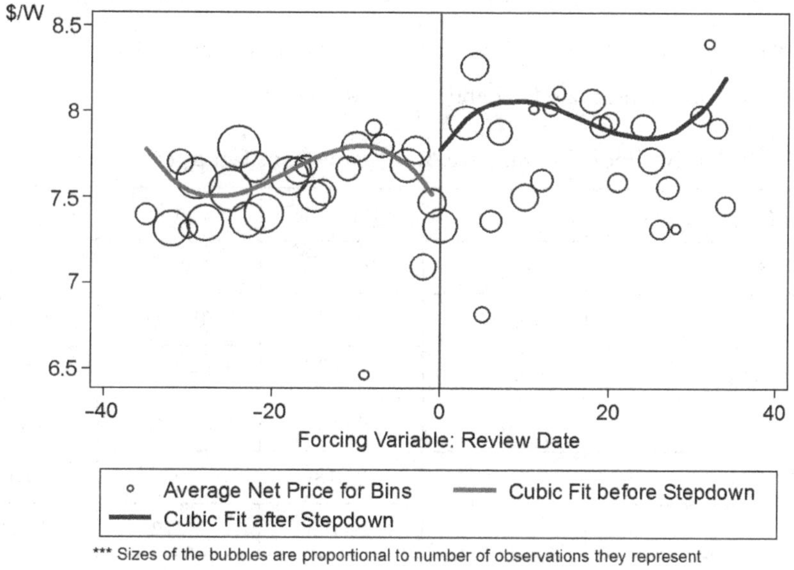

Figure 23 RD Graph of a Cubic Fit of Net Price: PG&E Stepdown 2~3

Table 10 summarizes the results for pass-through rates in PG&E when pooling all right stepdowns together and with four different orders of polynomials of the forcing variable as controls. For brevity, the review date on and after the stepdown is denoted by the subscript "+"; otherwise, by the subscript "−". Then different

① Other bandwidths were tried but showing no sensitivity.

② Other orders of polynomials produce pass-through rates varying from 71%~90%; neither of them was statistically significant due to the small sample within one stepdown.

polynomial orders are denoted by the superscript of the review date. The first row in Table 10 captures the pass-through rates(ignoring the negative signs and multiplying them by 100%). Fitting in different polynomial orders seems not to change the pass-through rate much, and all of the four coefficients are not significantly different from −1, i.e., a 100% pass-through rate. This is consistent with the descriptive analysis in Figure 19 and Figure 21(a). Also note that PG&E stepdown-level fixed effects are added in all the regression specifications. Since there are eight stepdowns for eight steps, seven dummy variables were added for the latter six stepdowns. This is because both rebate rate and net price have decreased over time; without limiting the variation into within-stepdown, it is easy to obtain a positive coefficient for the rebate variable. In addition, adding control variables such as system characteristics and social demographics barely changes the coefficients.

Table 10 Pooled Parametric RD Regressions Output for PG&E

DV: Net price($/W)	Linear	Quadratic	Cubic	Quartic
Rebate($/W)	−1.367***	−1.231***	−1.225***	−1.017***
	(0.178)	(0.172)	(0.175)	(0.183)
Review $date_+$	−0.005**	0.031***	0.058**	0.235***
	(0.003)	(0.009)	(0.026)	(0.059)
Review $date_-$	−0.004*	−0.018**	−0.039**	−0.068*
	(0.002)	(0.007)	(0.017)	(0.035)
Review $date_+^2$		−0.001***	−0.003	−0.031***
		0.000	(0.002)	(0.008)
Review $date_-^2$		−0.000*	−0.002	−0.004
		0.000	(0.001)	(0.004)
Review $date_+^3$			0.000	0.001***
			(0.000)	(0.000)
Review $date_-^3$			0.000	0.000
			(0.000)	(0.000)

Continuation

DV: Net price($/W)	Linear	Quadratic	Cubic	Quartic
Review date$^4_+$				−0.000***
				(0.000)
Review date$^4_-$				0.000
				(0.000)
Constant	9.015***	8.762***	8.699***	8.353***
	(0.227)	(0.215)	(0.205)	(0.212)
Stepdown Fixed Effects	Yes	Yes	Yes	Yes
N	12341	12341	12341	12341
Adj-R2	0.079	0.08	0.08	0.083
df_m	3	5	7	9

Note: A time window of 35 days was used; zip code clustered robust standard errors are reported in parentheses; DV = dependent variable; *$p<0.10$, **$p<0.05$, ***$p<0.01$.

②Nonparametric Model for Time Discontinuity

As in Eq. 28, the nonparametric model is approximated using a local linear regression model. The key to implementing this method is to select an optimal bandwidth(in number of days) to balance data efficiency and estimation bias. Similar to the parametric model, the local linear regression can be run for each stepdown or for all of them together.

Figure 24 shows the results for the pooled version of PG&E stepdowns. While the optimal bandwidth is around 5 or 6 days before and after the stepdowns, based on the Imbens and Kalyanaraman(2012) method,① different choices are used, with the corresponding bandwidth varying from 4 days to 2 weeks. Such short time alleviates potential selection bias concern in the sense that the decision period to adopt solar PV is generally in months(Rai and Robinson, 2013).

① The robust RD method proposed by Calonico et al.(2014) provided very similar answers in terms of bandwidth selection.

Figure 24 also shows results from four different regression specifications: ordinary least squares(OLS) with rectangular kernel weights, OLS with triangular kernel weights, quantile regression, and two-stage least squares(2SLS) with instruments for the rebate variable. The triangular kernel option gives more weight to observations close to the cutoff point, whereas the rectangular option treats all the observations the same. While quantile regression is less sensitive to outliers in observations, 2SLS is the appropriate approach to fuzzy RD designs.① Figure 24 strongly suggests that the pass-through rate is very close to −1, i.e., a complete pass-through rate; different bandwidths and specifications seem not to impact the results much. This adds confidence to the parametric results above, even with a much smaller time window here.

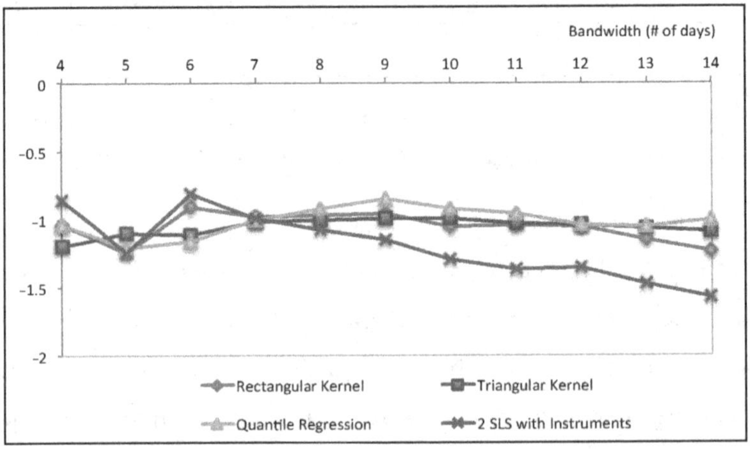

Figure 24 Nonparametric Results for the RD Design: Pooled PG&E Stepdowns

It is necessary to test the underlying assumptions for the time RD design before showing results for other utilities. The first assumption, the unconfoundedness assumption, is easy to test and perfectly satisfied if it is without crossovers; even with crossovers, fuzzy RD is able to tackle such violations. The second

① A small portion of PV systems are treatment crossovers; in other words, they receive different rebate rates than most others. The rebate rates are usually lower for them if they reserved before the stepdown date and higher after. Ideally, these systems can be excluded or the right rebate rate can be used as an IV for them.

assumption, of continuity and no manipulation, seems to be more challenging. Here, McCrary's(2008) density test was first adopted to see if the forcing variable has been manipulated or not. The idea of such a test is to see if there are significantly more observations on one side of the cutoff point than the other, which consists of a self-selection problem. This test is especially relevant owing to the potential announcement effect that attracts more people immediately before the stepdown date.

To implement such a test, one stepdown with the most significant announcement effect for PG&E(stepdown 6~7) was picked. During this stepdown, the daily reservation numbers increased the most immediately before the stepdown date. Figure 25 gives the density test results. The forcing variable density increased before the cutoff date, but its difference from the post-stepdown density is only marginally significant(with a p-value of about 0.09). The relatively high density before the stepdown may only have a quantity impact, with no significant influence on the installation price, as in Figure 20(a). Figure 25 also shows that there are data supports for all levels of the forcing variable, which improves the estimation efficiency of RD.

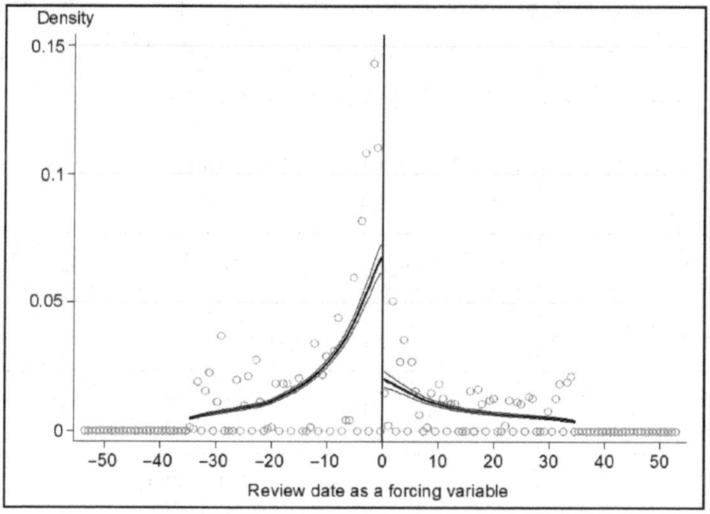

Figure 25 McCrary's Density Test for PG&E Stepdown 6~7

Note: p-value = 0.0899

One additional test is to make sure the control variables are balanced before and after the rebate stepdown. Still looking at PG&E stepdown 6~7, two sets of variables in Table 11 are compared via mean-difference tests: system characteristics and social demographics. During this stepdown, PV systems were very similar to each other based on all other system characteristics except for the(pre-rebate) price and the rebate rate. While the rebate rate was scheduled to decrease, there seemed to be no good reason for the pre-rebate price to differ before and after the stepdown(see the discussion around Figure 19). Fortunately, when all stepdowns are pooled together, such a difference in price starts to disappear, as indicated in Figure 21(a).

Looking at social-demographic variables, there are small disparities in several housing value and education categories. However, such results are mostly due to distributional density differences before and after the stepdown; in other words, more PV adopters come from relatively wealthy and highly educated areas before the stepdown than those from after. After the PV adoption density difference was removed, the social demographics related to PV systems grouped very tightly by zip code. The distributional difference in social demographics helps explain the difference in the pre-rebate price term to some extent. As demonstrated in Section 5.4.1.3, this disparity in price was a more serious problem for other utilities. Overall, there is a reasonable balance for PV systems in PG&E before and after the stepdowns, which reinforces the time RD findings above.

Table 11 Balance Test for Control Variables pre-PG&E and post-PG&E Stepdown 6~7

Variable	Difference	Variable	Difference
Net price($/W)	0.126	Household income ($45,000~$99,999)	0.003
Price($/W)	-0.295^{***}	Household income (⩾ $100,000)	−0.003
Rebate($/W)	-0.420^{***}	Housing value (⩽ $34,999)	0.002^{*}
System size(kW)	−0.063	Housing value ($35,000~$89,999)	0.003

Continuation

Variable	Difference	Variable	Difference
Third-party owned	0.003	Housing value ($90,000~$249,999)	0.031***
China module	0.017	Housing value (⩾ $250,000)	−0.030***
Micro-inverter	0.005	Less than high school	0.000
Thin-film	−0.002	High school without diploma	0.006***
Building-integrated PV (BIPV)	−0.002	Less than bachelor	0.019***
Household income (⩽ $24,999)	0.004	Bachelor degree or more	−0.019**
Household income ($25,000~$44,999)	0.002	Occupied housing units (in 10,000)	0.008

Note: *p<0.10, **p<0.05, ***p<0.01.

③Results for Other Utilities

In theory, the same methodology could be adopted for the other utilities as for PG&E. However, the distributional problem is more serious for the others, especially in the pre-rebate price. This phenomenon is fundamentally caused by the announcement effect(or pulling-forward effect), which literally created a different price distribution before and after the stepdown and thus the two significantly different average prices. Figure 26 conveys the idea. As an example, the figure shows the pre-rebate price distributions before and after SCE stepdown 6~7. During this stepdown, more systems fell into the price range between $6/W~$9/W before the stepdown than after, as indicated by the "peakedness" of the distribution. As a result, the average price appeared to increase after the stepdown, not because there were many more expensive PV systems in the post-stepdown period. Such distributional differences inflate the pass-through rate since the(seemingly) increased average price will be attributed to the results of rebate rate changes.

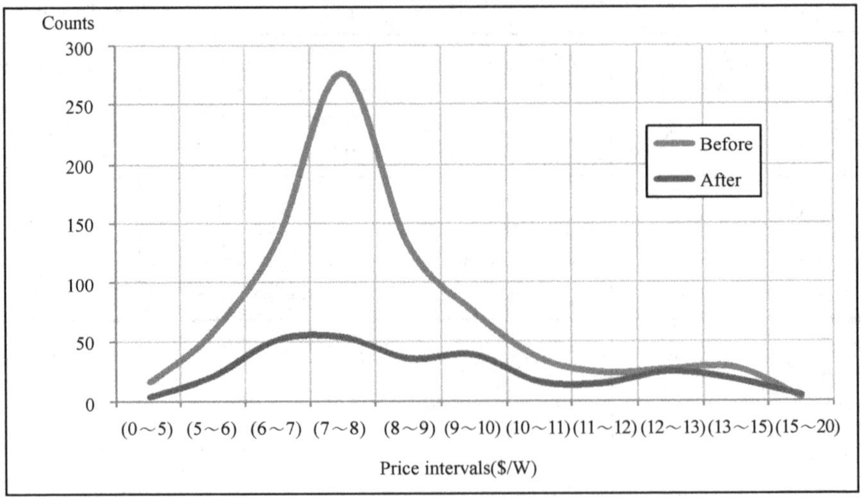

Figure 26 Distributional Differences in Pre-rebate Price before and after SCE Stepdown 6~7

Note: A time window of 2 weeks was used.

The McCrary's density test failed to reject the null continuity assumption in this case, since this test only looks at quantities instead of any price information. As a better option, the Kolmogorov-Smirnov equality-of-distributions test was used to test the distribution equality of the price before and after the stepdown, and it successfully rejected the null hypothesis. There are two approaches to counteracting the distributional differences in quantities, which brings about a problematic difference in the pre-rebate price. The first approach weights different price intervals by the inverse of the market share of those price intervals. It is essentially the idea of discarding any distributional differences for all price intervals, which seems problematic because, in the case of rebate decreases, the market response could be either on the average price(while ignoring the price distribution) or on the price distribution itself. For the latter response, basically, the market will adopt relatively more PV systems in a certain price range. However, this approach assumes away such a possibility.

The second approach is to introduce fixed effects into the RD framework, with each fixed effects term indicating a relatively broad price interval. In other words, instead of comparing all the prices at the same time in the original RD analysis, now I only compare prices within each price interval. This alleviates the distributional density problem. The underlying theory is that, even if installers could shift the price to some extent before the stepdown(probably lowering their prices) and then influence the customer distribution, it is "irrational" for them to shift the price across broad price categories, say by \$2/W(much larger than the rebate rate change for each stepdown). Thus, using price-interval fixed effects could remove such concern from the supply side. On the demand side, the high density in the price range of \$6/W~\$9/W could simply be because this was the favorite choice of most consumers during SCE stepdown 6~7. Similarly, using fixed effects will force the regression to ignore the quantity differences before and after the stepdown across different price categories.

Table 12 shows pooled parametric regression results for SCE, which work for SDG&E in similar ways.① The model specification with a cubic control function and price-interval fixed effects is as follows:

$$NP_{ijt} = \beta_1 \cdot s_{it} + x_{it} + x_{it}^2 + x_{it}^3 + x_{it}D_i + x_{it}^2 D_i + x_{it}^3 D_i + \theta_t + \delta_j + \varepsilon_{ijt} \qquad (33)$$

Eq. 33 is similar to Eq. 27, except that now there are stepdown fixed effects and price-interval fixed effects δ_j. Each δ_j is an indicator of a certain price range that is at least \$2/W.②

The results in Table 12 clearly show the advantages of the case with price-interval fixed effects(in the top panel)over the case without(in the bottom panel). Starting from the quadratic column, the former case demonstrates much higher consistency and is not sensitive to the polynomial orders, while the latter case produces counterintuitive results in the cubic and quartic columns. Further tests on the equality of coefficients of the rebate variable for the former case failed to reject the null hypothesis, while it is clearly not the case for the latter.

---

① The same technique can be applied to the nonparametric RD regressions, and results are available from the authors upon request.

② Specifically, I used six price ranges, including(0, 5],(5, 7],(7, 9],(9, 11],(11, 15], and(15, 20].

Table 12 Pooled Parametric RD Models for SCE with and without Price-interval Fixed Effects

DV: Net price($/W)	Linear	Quadratic	Cubic	Quartic
Rebate($/W)	-1.028^{***}	-0.919^{***}	-0.851^{***}	-0.820^{***}
	(0.064)	(0.071)	(0.074)	(0.076)
Price-interval fixed effects	Yes	Yes	Yes	Yes
Stepdown fixed effects	Yes	Yes	Yes	Yes
DV: Net price($/W)	Linear	Quadratic	Cubic	Quartic
Rebate($/W)	-1.146^{***}	-0.679^{***}	−0.206	0.028
	(0.222)	(0.236)	(0.237)	(0.240)
Price-interval fixed effects	No	No	No	No
Stepdown fixed effects	Yes	Yes	Yes	Yes

Note: $^{*}p<0.10$, $^{**}p<0.05$, $^{***}p<0.01$; DV = dependent variable.

(2)Geographic Discontinuity

When comparing two adjacent utilities, the distributional problem is a trivial issue based on Figure 20. However, two potential biases must be handled: initial condition bias and control group bias. Following the discussion in Section 5.3.2, the Ⅳ strategy is primarily used to separate the variation within the rebate rate variable. In addition, this approach is compared to the basic DID with RD designs. Difference-in-RD is inappropriate owing to the bias issue. Below the results are presented for the north geographic discontinuity, followed by the results for the south geographic discontinuity.

①North Geographic Discontinuity

Since SCE served as an excellent control group in the northern comparison with PG&E, it is relatively easy to apply the Ⅳ method directly. The Ⅳ used here is the interaction term(or the DID term) between the utility dummy and the stepdown dummy: the former is in geography and the latter in time. The IV strategy is very similar to DID plus RD, where the DID term is now used as an instrument for the variable of interest(rebate). The similarity can be seen clearly using the following equations:

IV Strategy: $NP_{it} = \beta_0 + \beta_1 s_{it} + \beta_2 D_i + \beta_3 U_i + \beta_4 x_{it} + \beta_5 (s_{it} x_{it}) + \theta_t + \varepsilon_{it}$

while $$s_{it} = \gamma(D_i U_i) + \eta_{it} \quad (34)$$

DID + RD: $NP_{it} = \beta_0 + \beta_1 (D_i U_i) + \beta_2 D_i + \beta_3 U_i + \beta_4 x_{it} + \beta_5 (s_{it} x_{it}) + \theta_t + \varepsilon_{it}$ (35)

where D_i is the stepdown indicator(1 for post-stepdown), U_i is the utility indicator(1 for PG&E), and $D_i U_i$ is the DID term. θ_t as usual is the stepdown fixed effects. Eq. 35 is instrumenting the rebate variable using the DID term. In addition, the forcing variable x_{it} is different from the time discontinuity case, and denotes the distance towards the shared border between PG&E and SCE.

To save space, results are shown below only for a 10-mile buffer and a local linear regression(i.e., nonparametric). Three slightly different specifications are compared in Table 13. M1 uses the DID term as the instrument for rebate, while M2 uses the rebate variable itself without instrumenting to show the potential bias there. M3 instead includes the DID term but not the rebate term(i.e., DID + RD). It seems reasonable to conclude that the other two specifications(M2 and M3) are problematic in terms of estimating the correct pass-through rate owing to the initial condition bias. Such a bias is more serious when pooling all three stepdown chances together. Because both the rebate and net price decrease over time, it becomes challenging to separate the true pass-through effect from the automatic correlation between these two variables from year to year. That explains the positive coefficient in M2 and M3. On the other hand, the rebate decrease within one stepdown is of most interest, which is captured by the DID term as an instrument along with the stepdown fixed effects. Thus, based on the specification in M1, relatively consistent and high pass-through rates are obtained. The coefficient obtained there is not statistically different from −1, i.e., a 100% pass-through rate.

Table 13 North Geographic RD Designs with Ⅳ Strategy:
Pooled Nonparametric Approach

DV: Net price($/W)	M1(Rebate with Ⅳ)	M2(Rebate)	M3(DID)
Rebate($/W)	−1.228***	0.562**	
	(0.010)	(0.026)	
PG&E * stepdown			0.243**
			(0.006)
PG&E	0.488***	1.510**	1.089**
	(0.154)	(0.061)	(0.060)
Stepdown	−0.164***	0.055	−0.123**
	(0.010)	(0.171)	(0.002)
Distance(feet)	−0.025***	0.003	−0.006
	(0.001)	(0.002)	(0.001)
Distance*rebate	0.011***	−0.005*	0.000
	(0.001)	(0.001)	(0.001)
Constant	10.058***	5.059**	6.683***
	(0.116)	(0.239)	(0.020)
Stepdown fixed effects	Yes	Yes	Yes
N	221	221	221
Adj-R^2	0.151	0.172	0.172
df_m	7	7	7

Note: Rebate variable is instrumented by the DID term; utility clustered robust standard errors are in parentheses; DV = dependent variable; *p<0.10, **p<0.05, ***p<0.01.

②South Geographic Discontinuity

The south geographic RD design is more challenging since multiple biases exist when comparing SDG&E and SCE. Owing to the control group bias, simply using the IV strategy as in the north geographic RD design would still result in a roughly 400% pass-through rate. To overcome this problem, more control variables must be introduced to explain the price drop in the control group.

Because the control group problem mostly occurred during SDG&E stepdown 7~8, this stepdown was separated from the other three SDG&E stepdowns. However, the methodologies used for each group are similar. A DID plus RD model was first run for both sub-samples, and the results were used to validate the IV strategy. In the former approach, the same model was run for both the pre-rebate price and the net price as the dependent variable. Then, the difference of the coefficient of the DID term was compared with the actual rebate decrease to obtain the pass-through rate. A regression(DID + RD) simply can be run for the pre-rebate price only and the pass-through rate from the DID coefficient inferred from there. However, when the coefficient is 0.4 and statistically insignificant, it becomes challenging to determine the resulting pass-through rate as 60% versus 100%. Such ambiguity can be avoided if the same model is run for the net price again and the difference is taken for the coefficient of the DID term.

More specifically, I run the following two regressions in parallel:

$$NP_{it} = \alpha_0 + \alpha_1(D_iU_i) + \alpha_2 D_i + \alpha_3 U_i + \alpha_4 x_{it} + \alpha_5(s_{it}x_{it}) + \alpha_6 Z_{it} + \theta_t + \varepsilon_{it} \quad (36)$$

$$P_{it} = \beta_0 + \beta_1(D_iU_i) + \beta_2 D_i + \beta_3 U_i + \beta_4 x_{it} + \beta_5(s_{it}x_{it}) + \beta_6 Z_{it} + \theta_t + \varepsilon_{it} \quad (37)$$

Then, the pass-through rate can be derived as$(\alpha_1 - \beta_1)/\Delta s$, which can be then multiplied by 100% to obtain the percentage. Comparing Eq. 35 in the North geographic discontinuity and Eq. 36 in the South geographic discontinuity, a set of control variables are added via Z_{it} in Eq. 36. These control variables include system size, TPO, China module, micro-inverter, thin-film, BIPV, and two additional installer-level control variables. One of the installer-level control variables captures the discounted installer experience within a county, while the other depicts the installation scale within a half-year time window. These variables are the major reasons why we see a control group bias in the South geographic discontinuity; however, there is no need to include them in the North case since no control group bias exists.

The rationale for the above way to derive the pass-through rate is that, possibly due to data randomness, the DID term in the pre-rebate price regression is different from zero(though insignificant); such randomness can be cancelled out by taking a difference of the DID term between the two regressions(Eq. 36 and Eq. 37). This difference term captures the adjusted impact on the net price term(by the impact on the pre-rebate price) from the DID term, which further dates back the rebate rate differences between the two utilities. As a result, the correct pass-through rate is obtained.

Panel A of Table 14 presents the results from the DID plus RD model, while breaking the four stepdowns by SDG&E into two groups: the first three and the last one(where the control group bias arises). The estimated pass-through rate in the first three stepdowns is 81.2%, while the pass-through rate for the last stepdown is 96.1%. Based on the obtained pass-through coefficient, the control group bias has disappeared. In a typical DID model, the coefficient of the stepdown dummy variable(not shown here) should be able to test such control group bias, which was shown to be insignificant and close to zero after including the control variable set Z_{it}.

Table 14 South Geographic RD Designs with IV Strategy

Panel A	DID + RD	
	First three	Last one
Price as DV	0.320	0.619
	(0.428)	(0.497)
Net price as DV	0.622	0.907
	(0.428)	(0.498)
Difference / rebate decrease	−0.812***	−0.961***
	(0.055)	(0.024)
Panel B	IV Strategy(Net Price as DV)	
1 IV	−2.056	−3.146*
	(1.316)	(1.849)

Continuation

Panel B	Ⅳ Strategy(Net Price as DV)	
3 IVs	−1.449**	−1.083**
	(0.674)	(0.509)
All IVs	−0.741**	−0.800***
	(0.334)	(0.292)

Note: *p<0.10, **p<0.05, ***p<0.01.

Panel B of Table 14 follows the approach in the north geographic RD designs, where an Ⅳ strategy was adopted. Owing to the control group bias, it seems that more IVs need to be added to account for such bias. In the "1 IV" case, only the DID term was used as an Ⅳ as done previously(Eq. 34). Two more terms were included in the "3 IVs" case: the utility dummy and the stepdown dummy.① Lastly, the "All IVs" case included all the right-hand-side variables in Eq. 36 as Ⅳ for rebate. Using results from Panel A as a baseline, the appropriate number of IVs seems to be between the "3 IVs" case and the "All IV" case. In other words, the Ⅳ strategy is able to bound the baseline results, an indication of its effectiveness. The intuition behind this approach is that, if some of these control variables can explain the control group bias in the pre-rebate price term, they should be used to explain the rebate variation too. Since both the pre-rebate price term and the rebate term equally appear in net price(the dependent variable), only accounting for the former(as in DID + RD) without accounting for the latter(using the same control variables) will bias the results again. On the other hand, wherever there is no control group bias, as in the north utility boundary, adding more control variables barely changes the key results.②

5)Conclusions

In this chapter, a quasi-experimental method, RD, is adopted to estimate

① So Eq. 28 now becomes $s_{it} = \gamma_1(D_iU_i) + \gamma_2 D_i + \gamma_3 U_i + \eta_{it}$. Similar logic applies to the "All IVs" case.

② Detailed results are available from the authors upon request.

the incentive pass-through rate for the CSI, the largest state-level solar incentive program in the United States. Both the CSI rebate-level stepdowns and the geographic discontinuity between utility areas were used as a basis for the RD designs. More importantly, RD was adapted to account for potential estimation biases. Overall, the findings indicate nearly complete pass-through rates for the CSI, though these may vary to some extent from one utility to another. Specifically, both the parametric and nonparametric approaches produced a pass-through rate around 100%, varying from 81.2% to 136.7% depending on the discontinuities, the utilities, the models, and the estimation approaches. This finding is consistent with findings in Dong et al.(2014).

A complete pass-through rate aligns with the qualitative observation that installers tend to consider CSI rebates as exogenous factors when making pricing decisions, and it is generally suggestive of a competitive market and a smoothly operating subsidy program. After all, the rebate decrease for each stepdown is relatively small; in other words, the incentive for installers to manipulate their pricing behavior and absorb part of the rebate level change is limited. Furthermore, the fast and transparent data sharing and publication by CSI should serve as an effective mechanism for monitoring installers' pricing behaviors. Conversely, installers need not reduce prices after the stepdown to attract customers, simply because it is more lucrative to sell the stepdown opportunity and acquire more customers immediately before the stepdown. After the stepdown, even with a much smaller customer base, installers can use the time and finish the system installations they sought before.

A complete pass-through rate suggests enough installers have been active in most local markets, but this does not mean these installers are equally cost efficient. Other evidence indicates a sizable difference in PV prices among different installers, suggesting that some level of installer consolidation may occur even with a complete pass-through rate. The PV-installation sector tends to have very low entry barriers, and installer sizes vary greatly. With significant peer effects for PV adoption(Bollinger and Gillingham, 2012; Rai and Robinson, 2013), small installers could simply follow the movements of large ones and leverage peer effects to generate leads and installations. However, this does not necessarily mean small installers are less cost competitive. A promising and competitive PV market will benefit the most cost-competitive installers after the industry-consolidation process, which is ongoing now.

Though this study finds—using multiple RD designs—a high level of incentive pass-through for CSI, it is important to be careful in generalizing these results to other programs and other states. A fundamental constraint of RD designs is the tradeoff between data availability and potential biases that introducing more data will incur. Since CSI is the largest PV incentive program, other programs may not be well suited to this analytical technique. Even for CSI, in some cases, multiple discontinuity opportunities had to be pooled together to produce good estimates. This is more challenging for smaller programs. Another limitation of this study is that, when the IV strategy is applied to address biases in this geographic discontinuity setting, the term is used only loosely; there is no endogeneity problem here, and the IV is only used to separate part of the variation in the key independent variable. Other researchers may use different methods to tackle this problem.

Chapter 6 Conclusion

Using a multi-faceted, multi-method approach,this dissertation has examined optimal incentive policy design and subsidy pass-through—questions of recurring interest in many areas of public policy and public economics—for solar PV. Specifically, I have studied the largest state-level PV incentive program in the United States: the California Solar Initiative(CSI). I first investigate the policy-making history and the policy design logic of the CSI, which guides the modeling strategies and the choice of methods across the chapters in this dissertation. I then study the CSI as an incentive policy design question in more detail from two different perspectives. The first perspective looks at optimal subsidy schedules for maximizing the cumulative PV installations under a budget constraint, whereas the second perspective dives into the redistribution question of who actually benefits from the subsidy, i.e. the incentive pass-through question. These two perspectives are complementary to each other in the sense that while certain policy design features of the CSI help explain the high pass-through rate, results on the incentive pass-through also suggest a smoothly operating subsidy program.

In addressing the above questions, I have used multiple methodologies. For the question of optimal subsidy schedules, I bring in Hamiltonian-type analytic solutions and compare them with computational results from dynamic programming. For the dynamic programming modeling, both a deterministic case and a stochastic case are considered. More specifically, a dynamic regression model of learning-by-doing is estimated to obtain time-varying learning coefficients for the stochastic case. I shift my methodological approach for the incentive pass-through analysis: structural modeling, fixed-effects regression analyses, and regression discontinuity designs are compared and found to be consistent with each other. More importantly, I have combined RD with fixed effect, difference-in-difference, and instrumental variables to account for potential estimation biases within the underlying empirical setting of CSI.

In the dynamic programming model presented in Chapter 3 I find that the optimal rebate schedule would start not at \$2.50/W as in CSI, but instead at \$4.20/W, and the effective policy period would be only three years instead of the realized period of six years. The steeper optimal schedule is due to the presence of(strong) penetration effects and(modest) LBD that exist during the CSI effective time. This optimal solution results in total PV adoption of 32.2MW, which is 8.1% higher than the total installed under CSI, using the same budget. Sensitivity analyses have shown strong robustness of the results to different parameter values, functional forms and even multiple policy goals. Furthermore, the resultant rebate schedule stimulates significantly more PV adoption(26.4%) compared to the CSI in a 'policy flexibility' scenario where rebates are adjusted in ten steps. On the other hand, and interestingly, the optimal schedule starts to look like the actual CSI in a 'policy certainty' scenario where the variation of periodic subsidy-level changes is constrained. Finally, introduction of stochastic learning-by-doing does not yield significantly different results compared to the deterministic case, due to relatively stable LBD dynamics from 2007 to 2009.

Regarding incentive pass-through, results presented in both Chapters 4 and 5 consistently show a nearly complete(100%) pass-through rate for CSI using different methods, though with some level of heterogeneity among California counties. The structural-modeling approach estimates county-level pass-through rates that vary from 92% to 103%, with a mean value of 99%. The reduced-form regression analysis tends to consistently find average pass-through rates ranging from 86% to 103% at the state level, with a county-level weighted average pass-through rate of 95%. Focusing on the inner 10th~90th percentile of reduced-form pass-through results at the county level, a range of 68% to 122% is estimated. The regression discontinuity designs further lend credibility to the finding of a nearly complete incentive pass-through rate. The estimated pass-through rates vary from 81.2% to 136.7%, depending on the discontinuities, the utilities, the models, and the estimation approaches used, with a central tendency around 100%. In other words, PV customers seem to have benefited fully from the provision of the upfront state-level incentives.

Combining findings from these two different perspectives for approaching the CSI, this dissertation is generally suggestive of a relatively competitive PV market in California and a smoothly operating subsidy program, with the incentives going to the intended recipients: PV customers. The flexible policy design in the megawatt triggering mechanism, the transparency and policy certainty provided upfront, and the commitment by the government, when all considered together, help explain the policy success in making California the pioneer of the U.S. solar market. Though the CSI has now wound down as final solar capacity targets have been reached, incentive programs of various types still exist in the U.S. and other countries. Thus, the historical performance of the CSI is relevant not only as an ex-post analysis in California, but potentially has broader policy implications for other solar incentive programs both nationally and internationally.

A robust understanding on how one policy works in practice helps inform other policy instruments that promote renewable energy technology deployment and address markets failures when they arise. The similarity between upfront rebates and performance-based incentives is high; once a PBI(or FiT) is guaranteed for a number of years, it can be regarded as upfront after discounting and assuming an average electricity generation value, as done in Lobel and Perakis(2011). On the other hand, the incentive pass-through question for the federal ITC has been analyzed before using similar methods(Podolefsky, 2013). One observation resulting from this dissertation is that the effect of the incentive on demand can be exaggerated by the existence of strong penetration effects, but that can only fully be studied in a dynamic modeling framework. In other words, allocating the same incentive in different years could result in different cumulative PV adoption in the end. Considering such interaction effects demands more research in the policy instrument comparison literature(Fischer and Newell, 2008; Pizer, 1999), which also tends to ignore the incentive pass-through perspective in evaluating different policy instruments.

Appendix

Seeking a solution that satisfies all the requirements of the CSI design and is close to the CSI final decision can be explored easily in the Excel Solver. Assume that the target for each step is Q_t, and the total budget is M. What CSI chooses is two series of rebate levels for government/non-profit(Gov) and residential/commercial(Res/Com): G_t and R_t, where takes values from 2 to 10, indicating each step except the first one. The target is: $\Sigma_t(0.2Q_t \times G_t + 0.8Q_t \times R_t)$, where 0.2 and 0.8 are the CSI-assigned capacity share for each sector. Now consider the constraints:

From CSI:

$$0.5 \leqslant G_{t-1} - G_t \leqslant 0.45,\ 0.5 \leqslant R_{t-1} - R_t \leqslant 0.45 \tag{A1}$$

$$G_{t-1} - G_t \leqslant 0.3,\ R_{t-1} - R_t \leqslant 0.3 \quad \forall t = 3, 4 \tag{A2}$$

$$R_{10} \geqslant 0.2 \tag{A3}$$

$$G_t - R_t \leqslant 0.75 \tag{A4}$$

From this chapter:

$$G_t - R_t \geqslant 0.5 \tag{A5}$$

$$R_t \geqslant max(R_{t-1} - 0.45, R_{t+1} + 0.05) \quad \forall t \in [5, 9] \tag{A6}$$

$$G_t \geqslant max(R_t + 0.5, G_{t+1} + 0.05) \quad \forall t \in [5, 9] \tag{A7}$$

$$R_9 - R_{10} \leqslant R_8 - R_9 \tag{A8}$$

The first four constraints are self-explanatory. Constraint(A5) is taking the final step as known and treating the difference between Gov and Res/Com($0.50 = $0.70~$0.20) as the minimal one. Constraint(A6) reconciles the possible conflicts from the two periods of constraint(A1) for R, whereas constraint(A7) enhances the lower bound of G_t further and combines constraints(A1) and(A5). The last constraint(A8) requires that the last stepping down for residential/commercial should be smaller than the previous one. These four additional constraints further pin down the resulting rebate levels in the ten steps as close as to the CSI policy. For example, the implication of constraint(A6) is that for the last several steps, since the step changes(i.e. $R_t - R_{t-1}$ and $R_{t-1} - R_t$) become smaller and smaller, it is highly possible that the lower bound for R_t depending on the later period(R_{t+1}+0.05) is bigger than that depending on the earlier period; the opposite for the first several steps. Since both lower bounds are derived from constraint(A1), this possible conflict can only be reconciled adding this new constraint(A6).

Table 15 first shows the CSI policy, then the recovered results from the Excel Solver after imposing more sensible constraints, and lastly another trial with the government and non-profit rebate levels fixed the same as in the actual CSI. Based on the recovered results, the rebate levels move around the CSI policy, except for the first few steps. Even with the rebate levels fixed at the actual CSI levels for the government and non-profit sector, the residential and commercial levels still cannot match the exact CSI policy arrangement.

Table 15 CSI Step-wise Incentive Level Recovery

CSI			Recovered			Fixing Gov
Gov	Res/Com	Target	Gov – 20%	Res/ Com – 80%	Budget	Res/Com
3.25	2.5	70	3.25a	2.5a	185.5	2.5
2.95	2.2	100	2.95	2.2	235	2.2
2.65	1.9	130	2.65	1.9	266.5	1.9
2.3	1.55	160	2.079063	1.579063	268.6501	1.525861
1.85	1.1	190	1.629063	1.129063	233.5220	1.095957
1.4	0.65	215	1.224929	0.724929	177.3596	0.645957

Continuation

CSI			Recovered			Fixing Gov
Gov	Res/Com	Target	Gov - 20%	Res/ Com - 80%	Budget	Res/Com
1.1	0.35	250	1.044169	0.363569	124.9223	0.346496
0.9	0.25	285	0.805511	0.281577	110.1136	0.273248
0.7	0.2	350	0.706177	0.2	105.4324	0.2
	Total	1750		Total	1,707	

a. This is assumed known without varying.

Bibliography

[1] Alexeeva-Talebi V. Cost pass-through of the EU emissions allowances: Examining the European petroleum markets[J]. Energy Economics, 2011, 33(6).

[2] Alizamir S, Véricourt F D, Sun P. Efficient Feed-In-Tariff Policies for Renewable Energy Technologies[J]. Operations Research, 2012, 64(1).

[3] Angrist J D, Lavy V. Using Maimonides' Rule to Estimate the Effect of Class Size on Scholastic Achievement[J]. Quarterly Journal of Economics, 1999, 114(2).

[4] Angrist J D, PischkeS. Mostly harmless econometrics: an empiricist's companion[M]. New Jersey: Princeton University Press, 2010.

[5] Angrist J D, Rokkanen M. Wanna Get Away? RD Identification Away from the Cutoff[J/OL].(2013-05-01)[2014-12-02]. http://economics.mit.edu/files/8554.

[6] Ansar J, Sparks R. The experience curve, option value, and the energy paradox[J]. Energy Policy, 2009, 37(3).

[7] Ardani K, Barbose, G, Margolis, R, et al. Benchmarking Non-Hardware Balance of System(Soft) Costs for U.S. Photovoltaic Systems Using a Data-Driven Analysis from PV Installer Survey Results[R]. Berkeley, CA: National Renewable Energy Laboratory, Golden, CO., 2012.

[8] Arrow K J. The Economic Implications of Learning by Doing[J]. Review of Economic Studies, 1962, 29(3).

[9] Arvizu, D, Balaya P, Cabeza L, et al. Direct Solar Energy[C]//Edenhofer O, Pichs-Madruga R, Sokona Y, et al. Renewable Energy Sources and Climate Change Mitigation. Cambridge, United Kingdom and New York, NY, USA: Cambridge

University Press, 2011:333-400.

[10] Azuela G E, Barroso L A. Design and performance of policy instruments to promote the development of renewable energy: emerging experience in selected developing countries[Z]. World Bank Working Paper, 2011.

[11] Barbose G, Wiser R, Bolinger M. Designing PV incentive programs to promote performance: A review of current practice in the US[R]. Berkeley, CA: Lawrence Berkeley National Laboratory, 2006.

[12] Barbose G, Darghouth N, Weaver S, et al. Tracking the Sun Ⅵ: An Historical Summary of the Installed Price of Photovoltaics in the United States from 1998 to 2012[R]. Lawrence Berkeley National Laboratory, Berkeley, CA, 2013.

[13] Barbose G, Weaver S, Darghouth N. Tracking the Sun Ⅶ: An Historical Summary of the Installed Price of Photovoltaics in the United States from 1998 to 2013[R]. Lawrence Berkeley National Laboratory, Berkeley, CA, 2014.

[14] Barnett P G, Keeler T E, Hu T W. Oligopoly structure and the incidence of cigarette excise taxes[J]. Journal of Public Economics, 1995, 57(3).

[15] Bass F M. A New Product Growth for Model Consumer Durables[J]. Management Science, 1969, 15(5).

[16] Bass F M, Krishnan T V, Jain D C. Why the Bass Model Fits without Decision Variables[J]. Marketing Science, 1994, 13(3).

[17] Battistin E, Rettore E. Ineligibles and eligible non-participants as a double comparison group in regression-discontinuity designs[J]. Journal of Econometrics, 2008, 142(2).

[18] Baumol W J, Bradford D F. Optimal Departures from Marginal Cost Pricing[J]. American Economic Review, 1970, 60(60).

[19] Baumol W J, Oates W E. The Theory of Environmental Policy[M]. Cambridge: Cambridge University Press, 1988.

[20] Bauner C, Crago C. Adoption of Residential Solar Power Under Uncertainty: Implications for Renewable Energy Incentives[C]//Agricultural & Applied Economics Association's 2013 AAEA & CAES Joint Annual Meeting, Washington DC, August, 2013.

[21] Beck F, Martinot E. Renewable Energy Policies and Barriers[M]// Cleveland C. Encyclopedia of Energy. San Diego: Elsevier, 2004.

[22] Bemmaor A C. Modeling the Diffusion of New Durable Goods: Word-of-Mouth Effect Versus Consumer Heterogeneity[M]//Kluwer, Gilles L, Gary L, et al. Research Traditions in Marketing. Dordrecht: springer, 1994.

[23] Bergin P R, Feenstra R C. Pass-Through of Exchange Rates and Competition between Floaters and Fixers[J]. Journal of Money Credit & Banking, 2009, 41(Supplement s1).

[24] Berry S, Levinsohn J, Pakes A. Automobile Prices in Market Equilibrium[J]. Econometrica, 1995, 63(4).

[25] Beshears J, Choi J J, Laibson D, et al. How Are Preferences Revealed[J]. Journal of Public Economics, 2008, 92(8 – 9).

[26] Besley T J, Rosen H S. Sales Taxes and Prices: An Empirical Analysis[J]. National Tax Journal, 1999, 52(2).

[27] Bettendorf L, Verboven F. Incomplete transmission of coffee bean prices: evidence from the Netherlands[J]. European Review of Agricultural Economics, 2000, 27(1).

[28] Bezdek R H. The environmental, health, and safety implications of solar energy in central station power production[J]. Energy, 1993, 18(6).

[29] Bird L, Reger A, Heeter J. Distributed Solar Incentive Programs: Recent Experience and Best Practices for Design and Implementation[R]. Berkeley, CA: National Renewable Energy Laboratory, Golden, CO, 2012.

[30] Black A. Payback On Residential PV Systems with Performance Based Incentives and Renewable Energy Certificates[J]. Solar, 2006, 6.

[31] Black S E. Do Better Schools Matter? Parental Valuation of Elementary Education[J]. Quarterly Journal of Economics, 1999, 114(2).

[32] Howard S. B. Modern Regression Discontinuity Analysis[J]. Journal of Research on Educational Effectiveness, 2012, 5(1).

[33] Bloom N. The Impact of Uncertainty Shocks[J]. Econometrica, 2009, 77(3).

[34] Bloom N, Bond S, Reenen J V. Uncertainty and Investment Dynamics[J]. Review of Economic Studies, 2007, 74(2).

[35] Bollinger B, Gillingham K. Peer Effects in the Diffusion of Solar Photovoltaic Panels[J]. Marketing Science, 2012, 31(6).

[36] Bollinger B K, Gillingham K. Learning-by-Doing in Solar Photovoltaic Installations[J/OL].(2013)[2013-12-01].http://kelley.iu.edu/BEPP/documents/Ken%20Gillingham-%20paper.pdf.

[37] Bresnahan T F. The oligopoly solution concept is identified[J]. Economics Letters, 1982, 10(1).

[38] Brownlees O, Perry G L. The effects of the 1965 federal excise tax reductions on prices[J]. National Tax Journal, 1967, 20(3).

[39] Burr C. Subsidies, Tariffs and Investments in the Solar Power Market[J/OL].(2012)[2013-10-06]. http://econ.arizona.edu/docs/JobMarket/burr_jobmarket12.pdf.

[40] Busse M, Silva-Risso J, Zettelmeyer F. $1,000 Cash Back: The Pass-Through of Auto Manufacturer Promotions[J]. American Economic Review, 2006, 96(4).

[41] Cabral L M B, Cabral M B. Equilibrium, Epidemic and Catastrophe: Diffusion Of Innovations With Network Effects[M]//Fagerberg J, Mowery D C, Nelson R R. The Oxford handbook of innovation. Oxford: Oxford University Press, 2005.

[42] Calonico S, Cattaneo M D, Rocio Titiunik. Robust Nonparametric Confidence Intervals for Regression-Discontinuity Designs[J]. Econometrica, 2014, 82(6).

[43] Carbonnier C. Who pays sales taxes? Evidence from French VAT reforms, 1987—1999[J]. Journal of Public Economics, 2007, 91(5).

[44] Carlsson F, Johanssonstenman O. Behavioral Economics and Environmental Policy[J]. Annual Review of Resource Economics, 2012, 4(1).

[45] Choudhri E U, Hakura D S. The exchange rate pass-through to import and export prices: The role of nominal rigidities and currency choice[Z]. IMF

Working Papers, WP/12/226.

[46] Clay K, and Werner Troesken. Further Tests of Static Oligopoly Models: Whiskey, 1882—1898[J]. Journal of Industrial Economics, 2003, 51(2).

[47] Cohen M, Lobel R, Perakis G. Consumer Subsidies with Industry Response for Green Technology Adoption[Z]. Working paper. 2013.

[48] Connor P V, Bürger L, Beurskens K, et al. Overview of RES-H/RES-C Support Options. D4 of WP2 from the RES-H Policy project[EB/OL]. University of Exeter, Exeter, UK.(2009)[2013-10-06]. www.res-h-policy.eu/downloads/RES-H_Policy-Options_(D4)_final.pdf.

[49] Cook T D, Campbell D T. Quasi-Experimentation: Design & Analysis Issues For Field Settings[R]. Chicago: Rand McNally College Pub. Co., 1979.

[50] Corts K S. Conduct parameters and the measurement of market power[J]. Journal of Econometrics, 1999, 88(2).

[51] Couture T. State Clean Energy Policies Analysis(SCEPA) Project: An Analysis of Renewable Energy Feed-in Tariffs in the United States(Revised)[R]. Golden, Colorado: Office of Scientific & Technical Information Technical Reports, 2009.

[52] CPUC(California Public Utilities Commission). California Solar Initiative Program Handbook[EB/OL].(2014)[2014-12-08]. http://www.gosolarcalifornia.ca.gov/documents/CSI_HANDBOOK.PDF.

[53] Créti A, Joaug J. Let the sun shine: Optimal deployment of photovoltaics in Germany[J/OL]. 2012[2013-10-06]. http://hal.inria.fr/docs/00/75/17/43/PDF/Cahier_2012-33.pdf.

[54] Davidson C, Steinberg D. Evaluating the impact of third-party price reporting and other drivers on residential photovoltaic price estimates[J]. Energy Policy, 2013, 62(9).

[55] Delipalla S, Keen M. The comparison between ad valorem and specific taxation under imperfect competition[J]. Journal of Public Economics, 1992, 49(3).

[56] Dell M. The Persistent Effects of Peru's Mining "Mita"[J]. Econometrica, 2010, 78(6).

[57] Dixit A K, Pindyck R S. Investment under Uncertainty[M]. New Jersey: Princeton University Press, 1994.

[58] Dixon H D, Somma E. The evolution of consistent conjectures[J]. Journal of Economic Behavior & Organization, 2003, 51(4).

[59] Dong C, Rai V. Optimal Subsidy Design under Uncertainty: A Dynamic Programming Evaluation of the California Solar Initiative[C]//New York: The 37 USAEE Conferences, 2014, June.

[60] Dong C, Wiser R, Rai V. Incentive Pass-through for Residential Solar Systems in California[R]. Berkeley CA: Lawrence Berkeley National Laboratory, 2014.

[61] Dow K, Downing T E. The Atlas of Climate Change: Mapping the World's Greatest Challenge [M]. 3rd Edition. Berkeley: University of California Press, 2011.

[62] Drury E, Denholm P, Margolis R. Impact of Different Economic Performance Metrics on the Perceived Value of Solar Photovoltaics[R]. Golden, Colorado: National Renewable Energy Laboratory, 2011.

[63] Drury E, Miller M, Macal C M, et al. The transformation of southern California's residential photovoltaics market through third-party ownership[J]. Energy Policy, 2012, 42.

[64] Due J F. The Effect of the 1954 Reduction in Federal Excise Taxes on the List Prices of Electrical Appliances[J]. National Tax Journal, 1954, 7(3).

[65] Energy & Environmental Economics. California Solar Initiative Cost-Effectiveness Evaluation[R/OL].(2011)[2012-12-01]. https://ethree.com/documents/CSI/CSI%20Report_Complete_E3_Final.pdf.

[66] EPIA. Global Market Outlook for Photovoltaics: 2014—2018[R]. Brussels, Belgium: European Photovoltaic Industry Association, 2014.

[67] Fertig E, Apt J. Optimal Investment Strategy in Low-carbon Energy R&D with Uncertain Payoff[C]//Austin, U.S. : the 31 USAEEE, 2012.

[68] Fischer C, Preonas L. Combining Policies for Renewable Energy: Is the Whole Less than the Sum of its Parts?[J]. International Journal of Environmental

and Resource Economics, 2010, 4(1).

[69] Fischer C, Newell R G. Environmental and technology policies for climate mitigation[J]. Journal of Environmental Economics & Management, 2008, 55(2).

[70] Fullerton D, Metcalf G E. Environmental controls, scarcity rents, and pre-existing distortions[J]. Journal of Public Economics, 2001, 80(2).

[71] Fullerton D, Metcalf G E. Tax Incidence[M]//Auerbach A J, Feldstein Ma. Handbook of Public Economics. Elsevier, 2002.

[72] Genesove D, Mullin W P. Testing Static Oligopoly Models: Conduct and Cost in the Sugar Industry, 1890-1914[J]. Rand Journal of Economics, 1998, 29(2).

[73] Gillingham K, Sweeney J. Market Failure and the Structure of Externalities[M]//Padilla J A, Schmalensee R. Harnessing Renewable Energy. Washington DC: RFF Press, 2010.

[74] Gopinath G, Itskhoki O, Rigobon R. Currency Choice and Exchange Rate Pass-Through[J]. American Economic Review, 2010, 100(1).

[75] Grembi V, Nannicini T, Troiano U. Do Fiscal Rules Matter? A Difference-in-Discontinuities Design[Z]. Working Paper, Bocconi University, 2011.

[76] Gron A, Swenson D L. Cost Pass-Through in the U.S. Automobile Market[J]. Review of Economics & Statistics, 2000, 82(2).

[77] GTM Research, Solar Module Spot Prices Hit Historic Lows in Q2 2014[R].(2014)[2013-12-01] http://www.greentechmedia.com/articles/read/q2-2014-lowest-module-spot-prices-ever.

[78] Gürtler M, Sieg G. Crunch Time: A Policy to Avoid the 'Announcement Effect' when Terminating a Subsidy[J]. German Economic Review, 2010, 11(1).

[79] Hahn J, Todd P, Klaauw W V D. Identification and Estimation of Treatment Effects with a Regression-Discontinuity Design[J]. Econometrica, 2001, 69(1).

[80] Heckman J J, Vytlacil E J. Econometric evaluation of social programs[M]// Heckman J, Leamer E. Handbook of Econometrics, Amsterdam: North Holland, 2006.

[81] Hendricks N P, Janzen J P, Dhuyvetter K C. Subsidy Incidence and

Inertia in Farmland Rental Markets: Estimates from a Dynamic Panel[J]. Journal of Agricultural & Resource Economics, 2012, 37(3).

[82] Henwood K. Subsidy Pass-through in Residential Solar Markets[R].(2014)[2013-12-01]. http://home.uchicago.edu/~/keithjhenwood/PTv5.pdf.

[83] Hicks J R. The Theory of Wages[M]. New York, NY: MacMillian, 1932.

[84] Hoff T E. Photovoltaic Incentive Design Handbook[M]. California: Clean Power Research Napa, 2006.

[85] Hughes J E, Podolefsky M. Getting Green with Solar Subsidies: Evidence from the California Solar Initiative[EB/OL].(2013)[2013-12-01]. http://spot.colorado.edu/~jonathug/Jonathan_E._Hughes/Main_files/PV_Subsidies.pdf.

[86] IEA. Deploying Renewables: Principles for Effective Policies[R]. Paris, France: International Energy Agency. OECD Publishing, 2008.

[87] IEA. Technology Roadmap: Solar Photovoltaic Energy[R].(2010)[2013-12-01] http://www.iea.org/publications/freepublications/publication/pv_roadmap.pdf.

[88] Imbens G W, Lemieux T. Regression discontinuity designs: A guide to practice[J]. Journal of Econometrics, 2008, 142(2).

[89] Imbens G, Kalyanaraman K. Optimal Bandwidth Choice for the Regression Discontinuity Estimator[J]. Social Science Electronic Publishing, 2012, 79(3).

[90] IPCC WG1. IPCC Special Report on Renewable Energy Sources and Climate Change Mitigation[R]. Geneva, Switzer: Working Group III of the Intergovernmental Panel on Climate Change, 2011.

[91] IPCC WG1. Climate Change 2013: The Physical Science Basis[R].(2014)[2014-12-02]. http://www.climatechange2013.org/images/report/WG1AR5_SPM_FINAL.pdf.

[92] IPCC WG2. Climate Change 2014: Impacts, Adaptation, and Vulnerability[R]. 2014[2014-12-02]. http://ipcc-wg2.gov/AR5/images/uploads/WG2AR5_SPM_FINAL.pdf.

[93] IPCC WG3. Climate Change 2014: Mitigation of Climate Change [R].(2014)

[2014-12-02] http://report.mitigation2014.org/spm/ipcc_wg3_ar5_summary-for-policymakers_approved.pdf.

[94] Ito K. Asymmetric Incentives in Subsidies: Evidence from a Large-Scale Electricity Rebate Program[J]. American Economic Review, Forthcoming, 2013.

[95] Jacob R, Zhu P, Somers M A, et al. A Practical Guide to Regression Discontinuity[Z]. Working Paper, 2012.

[96] Jaffe A B, Newell R G, Stavins R N. Environmental Policy and Technological Change[J]. Environmental & Resource Economics, 2002, 22(1-2).

[97] Jaffe A B, Newell R G, Stavins R N. A tale of two market failures: Technology and environmental policy[J]. Ecological Economics, 2005, 54(2).

[98] Jaffe S, Weyl E G. The First-Order Approach to Merger Analysis[J]. American Economic Journal-microeconomics, 2013, 5(4).

[99] Jamasb T, Köhler J. Learning Curves for Energy Technology and Policy Analysis: A Critical Assessment[M]//Grubb M, Jamasb T, Pollitt M G. a Low-Carbon Electricity System: Technologies, Economics, and Policy. Cambridge: Cambridge University Press, 2008.

[100] Kalish S, Lilien G L. Optimal Price Subsidy Policy for Accelerating the Diffusion Of Innovation[M]. Marketing Science, 1983.

[101] Karp L S, Perloff J M. Estimating Market Structure and Tax Incidence: The Japanese Television Market[J]. Journal of Industrial Economics, 1989, 37(3).

[102] Kemp R, Volpi M, Kemp R, et al. The diffusion of clean technologies: a review with suggestions for future diffusion analysis[J]. Journal of Cleaner Production, 2008, 16(1).

[103] Kim D, Cotterill R W. Cost Pass-Through in Differentiated Product Markets: The Case Of U.S. Processed Cheese [J]. Journal of Industrial Economics, 2008, 56(1).

[104] Kirkegaard J F, Hanemann T, Weischer L, et al. Toward a Sunny Future? Global Integration in the Solar Pv Industry[J]//World Resources Institute and Peterson Institute for International Economics, Washington DC, 2010, 47(WP10-6).

[105] Kirwan B E. The Incidence of U.S. Agricultural Subsidies on Farmland

Rental Rates[J]. Journal of Political Economy, 2009, 117(1).

[106] Klein A, Merkel E, Pfluger B, et al. Evaluation of different feed-in tariff design options[R].(2008)[2013-10-06]. http://www.feed-in-cooperation.org/wDefault_7/wDefault_7/download-files/research/best_practice_paper_2nd_edition_final.pdf.

[107] Köhler J, Grubb M, Popp D, Edenhofer O. The Transition to Endogenous Technical Change in Climate-Economy Models: A Technical Overview to the Innovation Modeling Comparison Project[J]. The Energy Journal Special Issue, Endogenous Technological Change and the Economics of Atmospheric Stabilization, 2006.

[108] Lanzi E, Wing I S, Carraro C, et al. Directed Technical Change in the Energy Sector: An Empirical Test of Induced Directed Innovation[C]//The Montreal: WCERE 2010 conference, 2011.

[109] Lee D S. Randomized experiments from non-random selection in U.S. House elections[J]. Journal of Econometrics, 2008, 142(2).

[110] Lee D S, Lemieux T. Regression Discontinuity Designs in Economics[J]. Journal of Economic Literature, 2010, 48(2).

[111] Lee D S, Moretti E, Butler M J. Do Voters Affect Or Elect Policies? Evidence from The U. S. House[J]. Quarterly Journal of Economics, 2004, 119(3).

[112] Levine M D, Koomey J G, Mcmahon J E, et al. Energy Efficiency Policy and Market Failures[J]. Annual Review of Energy & the Environment, 1995, 20(1).

[113] Lobel R, Perakis G. Consumer Choice Model for Forecasting Demand and Designing Incentives for Solar Technology[J]. SSRN Electronic Journal, 1748424, 2011.

[114] Lucas R J. Econometric Policy Evaluation: A Critique[J]. Carnegie-Rochester Conference Series on Public Policy, 1976:19-46.

[115] Macintosh A, Wilkinson D. Searching for Public Benefits in Solar Subsidies: A Case Study On the Australian Government's Residential Photovoltaic Rebate Program[J]. Energy Policy, 2011, 39(6).

[116] Mackay A, Miller N H, Remer M, et al. Bias In Reduced-Form Estimates

Of Pass-Through[J]. Economics Letters, 2014, 123(2).

[117] Marazzi M, Sheets N , Vigfusson R, et al. Exchange Rate Pass-Through to U.S. Import Prices: Some New Evidence[J]. International Finance Discussion Papers, 2005(49).

[118] Marion J, Muehlegger E. Fuel tax incidence and supply conditions[J]. Journal of Public Economics, 2011, 95(9).

[119] Maycock P D. The world photovoltaic market[R]. PV Energy Systems. 2002, January.

[120] Mazzola J B, Mccardle K F. A Bayesian Approach to Managing Learning-Curve Uncertainty[J]. Management Science, 1996, 42(5).

[121] Mazzola J B, Mccardle K F. The Stochastic Learning Curve: Optimal Production in the Presence of Learning-Curve Uncertainty[J]. Operations Research, 1997, 45(3).

[122] Mccrary J. Manipulation of the running variable in the regression discontinuity design: A density test[J]. Journal of Econometrics, 2008, 142(2).

[123] Mcdonald A, Schrattenholzer L. Learning rates for energy technologies[J]. Energy Policy, 2001, 29(4).

[124] Mendonça M. Feed-In Tariffs: Accelerating the Deployment of Renewable Energy[M]. London, UK: Earthscan, 2007.

[125] Meyer B D. Natural and Quasi-Experiments in Economics[J]. Journal of Business & Economic Statistics, 1995, 13(2).

[126] Nordhaus W D. An optimal transition path for controlling greenhouse gases[J]. Science, 1992, 258(5086).

[127] Nemet G F. Beyond the learning curve: factors influencing cost reductions in photovoltaics[J]. Energy Policy, 2006, 34(17).

[128] Nemet G F. Demand-pull, technology-push, and government-led incentives for non-incremental technical change[J]. Research Policy, 2009, 38(5).

[129] Nemet G F. Interim monitoring of cost dynamics for publicly supported energy technologies[J]. Energy Policy, 2009, 37(3).

[130] Painuly J P. Barriers to renewable energy penetration; a framework for

analysis[J]. Renewable Energy, 2001, 24(1).

[131] Parry I W H, Small K A. Does Britain or the United States Have the Right Gasoline Tax[J]. Discussion Papers, 2005, 95(4).

[132] Peltzman S. Prices Rise Faster than They Fall[J]. Journal of Political Economy, 2000, 108(3).

[133] Peng H. Optimal Subsidy Policy for Accelerating the Diffusion of Green Products[J]. Journal of Industrial Engineering & Management, 2013, 6(2).

[134] Peterman C J. Subsidy Pass-through for PV Customers[C]//Berkeley, CA: EI Camp, 2012.

[135] Pindyck R S. Uncertain Outcomes and Climate Change Policy[J]. Journal of Environmental Economics and Management 2012(63).

[136] Pizer W. Optimal Choice of Policy Instrument and Stringency Under Uncertainty: The Case of Climate Change[J]. Resource and Energy Economics, 1997, 21(3-4).

[137] Podolefsky M. Tax Evasion and Subsidy Pass-Through under the Solar Investment Tax Credit[J/OL].(2013)[2014-12-02]. http://www.colorado.edu/economics/papers/Wps-13/wp13-05/wp13-05.pdf.

[138] Popp D, Newell R G, Jaffe A B. Chapter 21-Energy, the Environment, and Technological Change[M]//B Hall, N Rosenberg. Handbook of the Economics of Innovation, Vol.2th, Burlington: Elsevier BV, Academic Press, 2010.

[139] Possajennikov A. The Evolutionary Stability of Constant Consistent Conjectures[J]. Journal of Economic Behavior & Organization, 2009, 72(1).

[140] Poterba J M. Retail Price Reactions to Changes in State and Local Sales Taxes[J]. National Tax Journal, 1996, 49(2).

[141] Rachapalli S R, Kulshreshtha P. Evolutionarily Stable Conjectures and Social Optimality in Oligopolies[J]. Theoretical Economics Letters, 2013, 3(1).

[142] Rai V, Robinson S A. Effective Information Channels for Reducing Costs of Environmentally-Friendly Technologies: Evidence from Residential PV Markets[J]. Environmental Research Letters, 2013, 8(1).

[143] Rai V, Sigrin B. Diffusion of Environmentally-Friendly Energy Technologies:

Buy vs. Lease Differences in Residential PV Markets[J]. Environmental Research Letters, 2013, 8(1).

[144] Reardon S F, Robinson J P. Regression Discontinuity Designs with Multiple Rating-Score Variables[J]. Journal of Research on Educational Effectiveness, 2012, 5(1).

[145] Reiss P C, Wolak F A. Chapter 64 Structural Econometric Modeling: Rationales and Examples from Industrial Organization[M]//James J H, Edward E L. Handbook of Econometrics. Amsterdam and Oxford: Elsevier, North-Holland, 2007.

[146] Rogers E. Effectiveness of Capacity-Dependent Rooftop Solar Subsidies: Lessons from California[Z]. North Carolina State University, Working Paper, 2014.

[147] Rosenbaum P, Rubin D. The Central Role of the Propensity Score in Observational Studies for Causal Effects[J]. Biometrika. 1983(70).

[148] REN21. Renewables 2013 Global Status Report[R].(2013)[2013-10-06]. http://www.ren21.net/Portals/0/documents/Resources/GSR/2013/GSR2013_lowres.pdf.

[149] REN21. Renewables 2014 Global Status Report[R].(2014)[2014-10-06]. http://www.ren21.net/portals/0/documents/resources/gsr/2014/gsr2014_full%20report_low%20res.pdf.

[150] Robinson B, Lakhani C. Dynamic Price Models for New-Product Planning[J]. Management Science. 1975(21).

[151] Sallee J M. The Surprising Incidence of Tax Credits for the Toyota Prius[J]. American Economic Journal: Economic Policy, 2011, 3(2).

[152] Sawin J L, Flavin C, Babu Y D, et al. National Policy Instruments: Policy Lessons for the Advancement & Diffusion of Renewable Energy Technologies Around the World[J]. Oil Gas & Energy Law Journal, 2004, 2(2).

[153] Schmalensee R. Appropriate Government Policy Toward Commercialization of New Energy Supply Technologies[J]. Energy Journal, 1980, 1(2).

[154] SEIA/GTM. U.S. Solar Market Insight Report: 2013 Year-in-Review[R]. GTM Research and Solar Energy Industries Association, 2014.

[155] Shadish W R, Cook T D, Campbell D T. Experimental and quasi-

experimental designs for generalized causal inference[M]//Experimental And Quasi-Experimental Designs for Generalized Causal Inference. Boston: Houghton Mifflin, 2002.

[156] Sherwood L. U.S. Solar Market Trends 2012[C]. Latham, NY: Interstate Renewable Energy Council, Inc., 2013.

[157] Shrimali G, Jenner S. The Impact of State Policy On Deployment and Cost of Solar Photovoltaic Technology in The US: A Sector-Specific Empirical Analysis[J]. Renewable Energy, 2013, 60(4).

[158] Shum K L. A General Technology Adoption Model of Solar Photovoltaic Under Feed-In Tariff Policy Incorporating Learning And Network Effects[J]. Journal of Renewable & Sustainable Energy, 2013, 5(4).

[159] Sijm J, Chen Y, Hobbs B F. The impact of power market structure on CO_2, cost pass-through to electricity prices under quantity competition – A theoretical approach[J]. Energy Economics, 2012, 34(4).

[160] Solomon B D, Georgianna T D. Optimal Subsidies to New Energy Sources[J]. Energy Economics, 1987, 9(3).

[161] Statista. Global investment in solar energy technologies from 2004 to 2013[R].(2014)[2014-12-02]. http://www.statista.com/statistics/186823/global-investment-in-solar-technology-since-2004/.

[162] Stavins R N. Environmental Economics[M]//Durlauf S N, Blume L E. The New Palgrave Dictionary of Economics, 2ed., UK: Palgrave Macmillan, 2008.

[163] Stern N. The effects of taxation, price control and government contracts in oligopoly and monopolistic competition[J]. Journal of Public Economics, 1987, 32(2).

[164] Timilsina G R, Kurdgelashvili L, Narbel P A. A Review of Solar Energy: Markets, Economics and Policies[J]. World Bank Policy Research Working Paper Series, Washington, DC, 2011.

[165] Timmins C, Schlenker W. Reduced-Form Versus Structural Modeling in Environmental and Resource Economics[J]. Annual Review of Resource Economics, 2009, 1(1).

[166] Tinbergen J. On the theory of economic policy[M]. Amsterdam: North Holland, 1952.

[167] Van B A, Gillingham K, Sweeney J. Learning-by-Doing and the Optimal Solar Policy in California[J]. Energy Journal, 2008, 29(3).

[168] Van Z B, Rabl A. The Learning Potential of Photovoltaics: Implications for Energy Policy[J]. Energy Policy, 2004, 32(13).

[169] Vaughan A, Harvey F, Gersmann H. Solar Subsidies to be Cut by Half[N/OL].(2011)[2013-03-07]. The Guardian. http://www.guardian.co.uk/environment/2011/oct/28/solar-subsidies-cut-half.

[170] Vavra P, Goodwin B K. Analysis of Price Transmission Along the Food Chain[J]. OECD Food Agriculture & Fisheries Working Papers, 2005(3).

[171] Vedenov D, Wetzstein M. Toward an Optimal US Ethanol Fuel Subsidy[J]. Energy Economics, 2008, 30(5).

[172] Verbruggen A, Fischedick M, Moomaw W, et al. Renewable energy costs, potentials, barriers: Conceptual issues[J]. Energy Policy, 2010, 38(2).

[173] Verdolini E, Galeotti M. At home and abroad: An empirical analysis of innovation and diffusion in energy technologies[J]. Journal of Environmental Economics & Management, 2011, 61(2).

[174] Vivid Economics. A Study to Estimate Ticket Price Changes for Aviation in the EU ETS[Z].(2007)[2014-12-02]. http://www.vivideconomics.com/uploads/reports/a-study-to-estimate-ticket-price-changes-for-aviation-in-the-eu-ets/Vivid_Econ_Aviation_Tickets.pdf.

[175] Vollebergh H R J, Edwin V D W. The Role of Standards in Eco-innovation: Lessons for Policymakers[J]. Social Science Electronic Publishing, 2013, 8(2).

[176] Wand R, Leuthold F. Feed-in tariffs for photovoltaics: Learning by doing in Germany?[J]. Applied Energy, 2011, 88(12).

[177] Weitzman M L. Prices vs. Quantities[J]. Review of Economic Studies, 1974, 41(4).

[178] Weyl E G, Fabinger M. Pass-Through as an Economic Tool: Principles

of Incidence under Imperfect Competition[J]. Journal of Political Economy, 2013, 121(3).

[179] Wing C, Cook T D. Strengthening The Regression Discontinuity Design Using Additional Design Elements: A Within-Study Comparison[J]. Journal of Policy Analysis & Management, 2013, 32(4).

[180] Wiser R, Bolinger M, Cappers P, et al. Analyzing historical cost trends in California's market for customer - sited photovoltaics[J]. Progress in Photovoltaics, 2007, 15(1).

[181] Wolfram C D. Measuring Duopoly Power in the British Electricity Spot Market[J]. American Economic Review, 1999, 89(4).

[182] Woodard F O, Siegelman H. Effects Of The 1965 Federal Excise Tax Reduction Upon The Prices Of Automotive Replacement Parts—A Case Study In Tax Shifting And Pyramiding[J]. National Tax Journal, 1967, 20(3).

[183] Wu H T, Colson G, Escalante C, et al. An Optimal US Biodiesel Fuel Subsidy[J]. Energy Policy, 2012, 48(48).

[184] Zaccour G. A Differential Game Model for Optimal Price Subsidy Of New Technologies[M]// Petrosjan L A, Mazalov V V. Game Theory and Applications II. New York: Nova Science Publishers, Inc. 1996.

[185] Zhang Y, Song J, Hamori S. Impact of subsidy policies on diffusion of photovoltaic power generation[J]. Energy Policy, 2011, 39(4).